Careers in Secretarial and Office Work

SEVENTH EDITION

GRAHAM HAYWARD

KOGAN PAGE
CAREERS
SERIES

First published in 1980
Seventh edition 1995

Kogan Page Limited
120 Pentonville Road
London N1 9JN

© Kogan Page Limited 1980, 1984, 1986, 1988, 1991, 1993, 1995

British Library Cataloguing in Publication Data

A CIP record for this book is available from the British Library.

ISBN 0-7494-1782-X

Typeset by DP Photosetting, Aylesbury, Bucks
Printed and bound in Great Britain by
Clays Limited, St Ives plc

Contents

Part 2

Foreword

by A E Reed, CBE, FCMA, FIPD, Founder and Chairman Reed Personnel Services plc, Professor of Enterprise and Innovation, Royal Holloway University of London.

It is a pleasure once again to commend this book to job-hunting secretarial and office workers. On this occasion I thought I would ask my secretary, Elaine Marks, for her views, having reached the top of her profession. This is what she wrote:

> Firstly, I should like to stress that I am proud of being a secretary. It is a career that I have enjoyed developing and I feel I have achieved a great deal. Not everyone, in any walk of life, will reach the top but there is a lot of satisfaction in secretarial work at all levels.
>
> I think of myself as Mr Reed's daytime manager, directly influencing his effectiveness. I am, among other things, his copywriter, diary keeper, telephone operator, travel agent, purchasing officer, banqueting manager, archivist, librarian, research assistant, party planner, customer service department and stand-by memory.
>
> The secretary's role is one of the most versatile positions in any organisation and there is a wealth of opportunity to add value to the job. The secretary, above all other employees, has direct access to the boss. What a tremendous opportunity to explain your latest idea or make suggestions for improvements elsewhere.

I wholeheartedly endorse those comments. If you are thinking of a career in secretarial and office work, you will find this excellent book opens the doors to a multi-faceted and rewarding job.

Alec Reed
Windsor, 1995

Introduction

Succeeding in a Business Environment

The object of this book is to suggest ways in which you can improve your chances of getting a job, of sharpening your competitive edge in relation to others. If this sounds daunting, the fact that you are reading this book is itself an indication that you understand the need to make yourself better prepared for the available jobs, for which you will be in competition with others.

If jobs are difficult to find at present, the scope for doing well in office work has never been greater. Every industrial company needs office workers, quite apart from such diverse activities as public services, banking, insurance, education and health services, publishing, travel and the law. The education and skills training available, examples of which are set out in Part 2, enable you to retrain or expand your competence as opportunity or interest suggest. There is no reason to suppose that what you do today will bear any relation to your career in ten years' time.

All marketable products have what are called *product benefits*, which are simply reasons why the public should buy them. In a sense, you are no different in this respect from a tube of toothpaste. You should consider why an employer should choose to employ you, rather than someone else.

For instance, all secretaries can type, by definition. Not enough of them can transcribe shorthand however, to meet the demand for shorthand typists. It follows that it is likely to make you more desirable to more prospective employers, if you can do shorthand. As a result, your choice of jobs will widen and the money you can earn will increase.

Equally, secretarial skills are particularly useful for building a career in many other fields. The ability to type and perhaps to take shorthand is vital to journalists, publishers, writers, the self-employed, insurance agents, marketing and advertising people and many others.

There are other skills, even more important, the mastery of which will definitely give you a competitive edge, not only at interviews, but in seeking promotion later. These are literacy and numeracy, both of which are now rare in persons under 50, and computer literacy.

The teaching of the English language, even at university level, is of extremely poor quality these days, for various reasons. A GCSE, an A level, or even a degree in English, unfortunately means little any more in terms of an ability to use the language properly and, of course, employers know this. Only those who have studied a foreign language at A level, or who speak English as a second language, will be likely even to understand the problem.

The importance of accuracy in English cannot be overstated. For a lawyer it might literally be worth millions of pounds. Language is a sign-system. It works because we all agree what a sign means. Any deviation from the agreed rules carries the risk that the signs will be misunderstood. Ideally, anyone should be able to read anything written in English and understand the sense of it. So written English should be clear as to meaning and simple in construction. Regrettably, all too frequently it is neither.

A short time ago, I received a sales letter which was virtually incomprehensible. I was so angry I analysed the mistakes, of grammar, syntax, spelling and wrong usages, it contained. There were 35 of them on one page. Recently, a major bank sent out a national mailing where the word 'except' was used, in bold capitals, when 'accept' was the word the sense required. Such errors excite ridicule and lose sales. They create a credibility gap in the public image of an organisation which is extremely damaging.

English is a flexible language, within limits. If someone says: 'Hopefully, he will arrive on Tuesday', we know that he actually means to say: 'I hope he will arrive on Tuesday' and is not referring to the chap's attitude of mind when he arrives. We know it is a frequent error to use 'disinterested', where the context demands 'uninterested', as is confusing 'affect' and 'effect'. There appears to be an almost complete breakdown in the use of the single inverted comma, denoting possession, or contraction, but we are usually able to understand what was intended (tomatoe's 45p, for instance!). All these things are still *wrong*. Avoiding such errors looks and sounds much better and, in business terms, reflects not merely on you but, more importantly, on your company.

Literacy has been largely replaced by semi-literacy, in which people hide behind long words and inaccessibility. They try to shut out the general public, with gobbledegook and jargon. Instead of referring to a red light, they might call it a 'vermilion luminescence'. The problem is that red and vermilion are not the same and neither are light and luminescence and the result of using such words is that many people do not understand what they hear or read, or become frustrated or irritated. That is, they receive the wrong signals. You will find words like 'cohort' used, when what is meant is 'group' or 'category'. Even the term *sign-system* is known as semiotics in 'academic' circles, which effectively shuts out all those who do not know the word.

In mathematics, it is similarly most useful to be able to solve a problem on the back of an envelope, in the middle of a meeting, without recourse to a calculator. Few can do it. Feeling comfortable with the four rules of arithmetic is no longer a standard skill, but it is still *needed*, every day.

There is a growing awareness of the need for these skills in modern business, reflected in courses in the English language and elementary mathematics, some of which I have highlighted in Part 2. If you can offer such skills, in addition to your other accomplishments, you should find job-hunting, and success in the job, much easier.

One last piece of advice: read books. You do not *have* to read the so-called classics, although it will always help if you do. Almost anything you read will be worth the effort, in giving you fluency in English. Also, if you do not already, read a daily 'broadsheet' newspaper, such as *The Guardian, The Independent, The Daily Telegraph, The Times*, or *The Scotsman*. Your increased grasp of current affairs and ability to develop and sustain argument will be noticeable. These things matter a great deal in job interviews and in a business environment.

Good luck!

NB: I have referred throughout to the typist or secretary as 'she' and the boss as 'he', but this should not be taken to imply sexual role-casting. There are plenty of female employers and male clerks and secretaries around.

Part 1

Chapter 1

Clerical Work

Office Clerks

Clerical work varies widely from office to office, depending on the size of the organisation as much as on what it does. In a small, general office, the clerk may well do everything from opening the mail to running the filing system, via making tea, balancing the petty cash and ordering stationery. In larger organisations, the work will be more specialised. Elementary knowledge of typing and arithmetic is always an advantage.

Filing systems are part of any clerk's life and these are now usually in the form of microphotographic and computerised systems. These are no more difficult to learn than the manual systems they are replacing and, of course, they are much quicker and easier to use. Most clerks will now be required to use a VDU (visual display unit), which looks like a small television set and is used to examine documents on file.

Clerks are employed in travel agencies, airline booking offices, road transport companies, department stores, solicitors' and accountants' offices: the opportunities are endless, as are the chances for promotion within the organisations concerned.

Local government and government departments, the National Health Service, the police and the armed forces all employ large numbers of clerks, often dealing directly with the public. Whatever field you choose, the work will always involve processing forms, dealing with correspondence and keeping detailed records.

Wages and Accounts Clerks

If you are good at maths, it is worth remembering that all organisations have wages and accounts clerks. You will probably have to take a PC (personal computer) course, although many companies will offer in-house training.

Wages sheets are quite complicated: hourly rates, piecework, holiday and sick pay entitlement, overtime, bonuses and expenses, are all elements of pay which vary with each individual, as do tax (PAYE), national insurance and pension deductions. Wages paid in cash require money to be withdrawn in the right denominations from the bank.

Accounts clerks have to ensure that money is collected and bills paid in the right ratio, to ensure the company's cash flow is correctly maintained. Purchase and sales figures, together with running expenses, have to be collated and the financial state of the company continually monitored, for the use of management and the company's accountants. You will need to understand how to prepare and use computer spreadsheets, which are electronic accounting tools.

Qualities Needed

- A methodical mind
- A liking for routine and order
- A pleasant manner and willingness to take orders
- An interest in improving your education, by day-release or evening classes.

Checklist of a Typical Clerk's Duties

- Open and distribute incoming mail
- Deal with outgoing mail
- Operate the photocopier and fax (see Chapter 6)
- Operate the filing system
- Process orders and remittances received by mail
- Keep the petty cash account for tea/coffee and other small items
- Take cheques and cash to the bank
- Answer the office telephone, take messages and help customers with their queries.

Training

It is possible to start straight from school, at 16, as the office junior, but it is an advantage to have taken commercial subjects at school, or to take a commercial or office-technology course at your local CFE (College of Further Education). Wages and accounts clerks will be expected to have at least GCSE Grade C maths. Further training at work is commonplace, particularly on office machinery, since systems and types of machines vary considerably.

You should certainly visit your local Careers Guidance Office before you do anything else. They can tell you about Training Credits, advise you about the best courses to take, explain about National Vocational Qualifications (NVQs) (or SVQs in Scotland) and even help you to find work. Your local Careers Service will be in the telephone book, either under that heading or the Local Education Authority, which is typically the County Council.

Courses

The National Council for Vocational Qualifications has prepared a comprehensive choice of courses, at different levels of competence, to suit every requirement in clerical work and to enable individuals to improve and broaden their skills as they wish. CFEs offer these courses, as well as their own and those of various national examining bodies, such as the Business and Technology Education Council (BTEC), London Chamber of Commerce and Industry (LCCI), Pitman Education Institute (PEI) and Royal Society of Arts (RSA).

Courses combine on-the-job, day-release and block-release study, especially for junior employees and trainees involved in clerical, secretarial and other office-based work.

The Scottish Vocational Education Council (SCOTVEC) offer the equivalent range of courses in Scotland.

Career Development

There are quite literally no limits, save your own ability and ambition, to a career in the business world. Many of the top finance and administration directors, to say nothing of managing directors, in British industry today started their working lives as office juniors.

Chapter 2

Typists and Secretaries

The advent of the microcomputer, or word processor (WP), as it is called, has completely revolutionised the role of secretarial staff. Fewer and fewer offices now use even electric typewriters, which were *the thing* only a short time ago. Electronic typewriters, which have many microcomputing functions, and word processors are now commonplace. Where does that leave the aspiring typist?

Word Processors and Software

Most word processors use the QWERTY typewriter keyboard, which is the same as the one our grandmothers learnt on, so you can master the basic skill by learning to type on any typewriter you can find. CFEs all offer WP courses, as do private secretarial colleges. Once you can type, learning to use a WP takes no more than a week. There are several different sorts of WPs, but they all do basically the same thing and once you have learned to use one, you can switch to another after a day or two of familiarisation. The most important aspect of word-processor training is the 'software'. The names you are most likely to hear at the moment (they change all the time) are Word for Windows, Microsoft or WordPerfect 5.1. Many companies arrange for in-house switch training for WPs and software and major employment agencies, such as Alfred Marks, Brook Street, Manpower and Reed, offer such conversion training as a service for their temps and client companies. (See Chapter 5.)

Shorthand

The other skill you need is shorthand. A recent decline in demand for shorthand means that there is now a shortage of shorthand secretaries, while the need for them has risen sharply again. As with any other service, shortage × high demand = rise in price, and there is no doubt that a good shorthand typist is in relatively high demand, even in these depressed times. All local colleges will offer shorthand and/or speedwriting courses.

The Pitman 2000 or Teeline systems are typical examples and excellent for the beginner. They are quite adequate for most shorthand needs and are much easier to learn than the advanced Pitman New Era. The disadvantage of the easier systems is that most people cannot achieve very high speeds with them, although the standard 80wpm is well within reach. (The Pitman 2000 is designed so that you can move straight from it into the New Era if you wish to later.) Systems such as Pitmanscript and Speedwriting are easier still but also slower.

Audio Typing

Most typists will need to do some audio typing from time to time, although this system is used much less than it was. It involves listening to a tape through headphones and typing documents from that. The main problem with it is that most managers will dictate as they think and make changes after you have typed their first thoughts! With a WP this is no problem: you type everything and then delete what is wrong. In the past it drove secretaries to despair.

Word Processing

If you are new to word processing you will find the advantages of a WP for a typist are numerous. Many have a spelling check function, for a start! Corrections and changes in the script can be made at the touch of a button, so all your work looks good and there is no tedious retyping if anything has to be changed. The style and presentation of a document is done by the machine, once you have set it, so your work can look very professional, even when you are still learning. A WP works faster than a typewriter, so you will be quicker than you thought.

While accuracy and clear thought are always important for any typist, a WP allows you to check your work and rethink what you have written, before presenting it to your boss. This is particularly helpful where you are given a vague instruction, such as: 'Write to Bloggs and tell him we can't possibly do this,' or a long report with lots of scratchings out and arrows moving things about, together with various illegible hieroglyphics in the margins – all part of a typist's life.

Typists and Shorthand Typists

Some companies use a pool system, where work is allocated to particular typists through a supervisor. In others, a shorthand typist might work for a small group of people. In the first case, you work mainly with other typists, while working for a small group of managers is quite likely to involve starting as general dogsbody and carving a niche for yourself by your own efforts.

Working in a small office or for a small group enables you to use your initiative, to suggest changes, to grasp something of company policy and perhaps help to shape it. If you are good, management will come to value your judgement, tact and ability to handle people as well as your technical skills.

Secretaries

A secretary is literally one who knows (and keeps) secrets. This is about as near to a definition as you can get. The line between shorthand typist and secretary, as between secretary and personal assistant, is blurred by such things as an executive's self-importance, the need to make a job sound attractive, or simply to save money. It follows that *you* should be clear in your own mind what it means to *you*. In this chapter, we will deal with junior secretaries, and cover the top jobs and the more unusual ones in the next.

The most important aspect of a secretary's job is that she will work for one person, or at most two. She will therefore inevitably be drawn close to her boss's life and find her first loyalty is to the boss rather than the company. She will have to behave discreetly with her friends in the company, keeping quiet about confidential information, yet remaining on easy terms with them in her capacity as the boss's eyes and ears.

Most secretaries act as a filter between their bosses and incoming telephone calls or visitors. Tact and diplomacy, an easy manner and willingness to help people, are all vital attributes of the good secretary. She must decide in mid-telephone call whether to put the caller through, stall for time, interrupt a meeting, pass the call elsewhere or endeavour to deal with the matter herself. If she gets it wrong, her decision can be very expensive or awkward but it is what she is paid to do. The most important thing to remember in this connection is, if you promise to call back, you must do so, even if it is to report you are still unable to complete the matter.

A secretary is expected to deal with most routine matters herself. Where the boss's decision is needed, she will try to find out all the facts, so that she can present the problem and perhaps a suggested means of dealing with it, for her boss's consideration. She usually makes travel arrangements and always keeps a diary, makes and breaks appointments and often ensures he remembers his wife's and children's birthdays and his wedding anniversary.

Company executives are frequently under a good deal of pressure, some of which rubs off on the secretary. Coolness under fire, a reasonably thick skin, quick thinking and quiet determination are all important.

If it sounds as though a secretary has to be a paragon of all the virtues, you have got the picture! It is a most important job, requiring dedication and enthusiasm. It can be very rewarding and is often highly paid. It can in turn be great fun or screamingly frustrating.

Many people find being a temporary secretary suits them. Temping is usually arranged through employment agencies. The advantages are that you have more choice of where and when you work; that you do a variety of different jobs; that you gain the help and support of your local agency and that you have an opportunity to find a company you really like. (Many temps end up working permanently for a company they originally temped for.) The disadvantages are that you keep having to learn new office procedures and where the stationery is kept, in a few minutes before starting work; that you have to get to know new people every week or so (but you do become confident quickly) and that you do not always have a job to go to, if work is short.

Qualities Needed by Typing and Secretarial Staff

- A good command of written English, particularly grammar and spelling
- A liking for routine and order
- The ability to mix well and understand people
- Common sense
- A cool, unflappable temperament
- The ability to work fast and accurately
- The confidence to use your initiative

- A sense of responsibility
- Discretion
- Punctuality
- Flexibility, concerning working late, for instance.

Checklist of Typical Secretarial Duties

- Opening and sorting the mail
- Dealing with routine correspondence
- Taking dictation
- Sending out the mail
- Filing
- Answering the telephone. Taking messages. Dealing with routine matters. Making sure the caller speaks to the appropriate person. Shielding the boss from unnecessary calls
- Looking after visitors
- Keeping a diary
- Making travel arrangements. Making sure the boss's passport is valid. Booking, paying for and obtaining tickets
- Arranging meetings. Typing the agendas. Taking accurate minutes and distributing them
- Keeping abreast of company activity. Reading trade newspapers and magazines
- Keeping a library of useful information, such as:
  telephone numbers; English usage, such as spelling etc; correct forms of address; train and plane timetables; hotels, travel hire firms and garages; restaurants, banqueting and conference centres; trade and professional publications; competitor information; government departments; legal and medical information.

Training

Ideally, a budding shorthand typist should take a one-year commercial or secretarial course at a CFE. If not, you will need to attend an intensive secretarial college, although a visit to your local Careers Guidance Office may be helpful first, see page 17. You will need shorthand at 80/100wpm, typing at 35/40wpm, and the ability to use a word processor, before you can seriously look for work. You should also have a reasonable command of English.

There are numerous qualification courses available, including BTEC and SCOTVEC awards, RSA, Pitman and London Chamber of Commerce and Industry, all of which can cover typing, shorthand and word processing, as well as business and finance studies. See Chapter 7, page 43 and following.

There is no specific training for a secretary, although there are numerous courses available which you would find useful, notably the Secretarial Skills option in the BTEC National Award and the awards of the Royal Society of Arts, the London Chamber of Commerce and Industry and Pitman. Details of these and other courses are also covered in Chapter 7.

Chapter 3
Personal and Specialist Secretaries

This chapter is mainly for those with more advanced qualifications or experience in other fields, although it will also serve to show the scope available in a secretarial career to those able or willing to fly high. Some jobs are closely defined: Legal Secretary, for instance. Others are notoriously vague. A Personal Assistant, Private Secretary, Executive Secretary, Executive Assistant, Administrative Assistant/Secretary or Secretary is actually the same thing and, whatever she is called, her job may be anything from highly paid executive to glorified gofer. (Gofer this, gofer that, in the American idiom.) What we mean here is a senior secretary, exemplified perhaps by Miss Moneypenny in the Bond films.

Senior Secretary

A senior secretary does all the things described in the previous chapter, except that she probably does them faster. Her shorthand is almost certainly Pitman's New Era, at perhaps 120wpm. She will type at 70/80wpm. She will quite possibly have at least one secretary of her own and will move among junior and middle executives and their staff as a figure to inspire awe. She will earn between about £15/20,000 and £30,000 or more, per annum, depending on the job and/or its location. She will be valued at least as much for what she thinks and knows as for what she types. She will certainly be over 30 in order to have the necessary experience to do the job.

The ability to communicate, often in highly charged office political situations, is essential. The senior secretary must be able to guess what her boss would think, say and do in any given circumstances. At the same time, she has to remember that she is not the boss herself and must not give herself airs which might make his job more difficult. Self-effacement is part of the job. She must be seen as the approachable side of her boss, as charming and interested and sensitive. It is a difficult balance to keep, which is why top secretaries are expensive. As top secretary Elaine Marks has put it:

> As the boss's filter, the secretary will often be the first point of contact with the customer. The initial responsibility of project-ing the right image and, indeed, nurturing the customer, will rest firmly at the secretary's door. Tact, lucidity and patience are prerequisites at this stage. Subsequently, you may need to demonstrate an understanding of how your company works, how your boss thinks and how you are going to satisfy your customer's demands.

In some posts, a secretary will often accompany her boss on business trips, at home and abroad. Maybe she will act as hostess to his business guests. In these cases, social graces will be important, for she must be as much at ease with presidents of multinational corporations as with the junior typists back home. She may even have to know how to deal with the press. Many speak one or more foreign languages. None work from nine to five, five days a week, except when things are quiet.

Training
The Royal Society of Arts offers a Higher Diploma in Administra-tive and Secretarial Procedures, intended for top-level personal secretaries or assistants, covering the background knowledge required and including assessment on the job. The London Chamber of Commerce and Industry offers a Private Secretary's Certificate, for secretaries to middle and senior managers, and a postgraduate Private and Executive Secretary's Diploma, for those with a senior appointment in secretarial or information-based management. The LCCI Diploma carries eligibility for membership of the Institute of Qualified Private Secretaries. Details of the latter organisation can be obtained from: Mrs N Harris, 68 Longmoor Road, Long Eaton, Nottingham NG10 4FP; 0115 973 3235. Both bodies regard experience as a prerequisite.

Specialist Secretaries

The requirements for a specialist secretary are not so much remarkable expertise in the secretarial role as particular skills or interests that can be put to secretarial use.

Farm Secretary

A farm, or agricultural secretary probably works for several different farmers on a part-time basis, since few farmers need enough help to justify a full-time secretary. There is usually little typing required. Most of the work is administrative: bookkeeping, VAT, wages and PAYE, preparing the farm accounts. You need to know about all these things and to be quite happy and confident working alone, since few farmers have the time to help, or the knowledge to be of much assistance if you are stuck.

Training

For a list of the colleges approved by the Institute of Agricultural Secretaries, offering specialist courses on this subject, usually lasting two years, see page 79. Or contact your Careers Service for information.

Legal Secretary

Legal secretaries are employed in solicitors' or barristers' offices, so the needs for absolute discretion and fast, accurate typing are paramount.

Understanding of legal terminology and of how and why legal documents are set out is important, although the word processor, with its memories and specialist functions, to say nothing of ease of correction, has taken an enormous amount of the repetitive work out of the job. Legal secretaries often specialise in a particular area of the law, such as criminal, litigation, property, etc, and there are agencies which specialise in placing such people in suitable jobs.

Training

Many legal secretaries start as office juniors and work up. Since this is a field where practical experience is of great importance, such a career structure has much to recommend it. Alternatively, you can qualify through one of the ILEX courses run by Colleges of Further Education (see page 76).

Medical Secretary

A medical secretary may work for the local GPs, in a health clinic or hospital, or for a consultant. She deals with confidential records, reports, lecture notes, etc, as well as the administration of the practice, such as waiting-lists, monitoring hospitalisation and after-care and telephone calls. She will need to understand basic medical terms and be good at spelling and reading indecipherable writing. Familiarity with the National Health Service and social services departments, as well as the local Health Authority are obviously essential. Working for a GP or consultant involves more contact with patients than working in hospital administration and tact, gentleness and a friendly, relaxing manner are important here.

Training
Many colleges offer specialist courses, including the two-year course for the Diploma of the Association of Medical Secretaries (see page 80).

Bilingual Secretary
How much a bilingual secretary uses her language(s) depends very much on the job or the company she works for. In some jobs you might hardly use it at all, only in translating the odd letter or making phone calls abroad. In others, where a firm does a lot of business abroad, you may have to translate incoming mail and compose replies, act as interpreter for foreign visitors, read foreign journals and even, occasionally, accompany the boss abroad.

If you have the relevant shorthand, there are opportunities for working abroad, though previous experience is often required by international organisations. The scope for such work is set to increase with our involvement in the European Union.

Training
Many colleges offer specialist qualifications, including the Royal Society of Arts and London Chamber of Commerce and Industry awards. Courses usually take two years and entry requirements in languages are GCSE/GCE O level minimum.

Chapter 4
Applying for a Job

There are four ways in which you can apply for a job: at a Jobcentre, whose address and telephone number you will find under 'Employment Service' in the telephone directory; through an employment agency (see next chapter); by answering newspaper advertisements; or by calling directly on a prospective employer. The advantage of the third and fourth is that you can go for jobs that take your fancy. In practice, you may well try all four.

You will need at least two referees, from school or college or previous employers, for instance. Make sure you ask their permission before you write down their names, with initials, titles and addresses.

The Application

Always remember you make a job application to get an interview, not the job. So everything you write or say must be aimed at an interview. Be precise, be brief, say nothing you are not asked to say.

Often, an advertisement will ask you to telephone in the first instance. Before doing so, make a brief note, like this: 'Sue - typist - *Evening Argus* - appointment?' ie: 'Hello, my name is Sue Brown. I am ringing in reply to your advertisement for a typist in the *Evening Argus* today and wonder if I may make an appointment to see you.' You have told them who you are, what job you are after, where it was advertised (they may have several job adverts running at once), and what you want from them. You sound polite but crisply efficient. If you do not make a note you may get muddled and if you write it out in full it will be apparent that you are reading it and you will sound terrible!

The personnel or human resources department will either send you an application form, ask you to come in, or ask you a few questions first – how old are you – what work have you done – what did you do at school – what qualifications do you have? As a result of your answers to those questions they will either proceed with your application or explain why you are not suitable. If they are not interested, do not despair, *think*! (Are you flying too high for your age/qualifications? Would you be better off getting help from an agency? Did you say the wrong thing?) But, before you telephone, make a list of likely questions and decide your answers to them. Have your CV beside you. If they decide to interview you over the phone initially, you must plan as you would for a face-to-face encounter (see below).

If you write a letter, make this brief and enclose a CV. If possible, type both of these, especially if you are applying for a secretarial job. If you write in longhand, use good quality writing-paper and write clearly, without any corrections. In both cases, do a rough draft and correct it first. Here is a sample:

---

28 Fore Street
Marton MN4 1CV

Tel: 0123 764829

15th June 1995

Ms H Williams
Prosser & Co
Quality Works
Worsthall WO1 4PQ

Dear Ms Williams

I wish to apply for the post of Junior Typist, advertised in today's *Evening Argus*.

I enclose a CV for your consideration and would like to add a few details to support my application.

Since leaving school, I have been practising my typing and learning shorthand and have completed a Word for Windows course.

I am available for interview at most times during working hours and look forward to hearing from you.

Yours sincerely

Susan Brown (Miss)

Enc.

Curriculum Vitae

Here is a typical CV. You can get help with yours at the Jobcentre and many employment agencies (see next chapter).

<table>
<tr><td colspan="2" align="center">CURRICULUM VITAE</td></tr>
<tr><td>Name:</td><td>Susan Brown</td></tr>
<tr><td>Address:</td><td>28 Fore Street, Marton</td></tr>
<tr><td>Date of Birth:</td><td>6 June 1977</td></tr>
<tr><td>*Driving Licence:</td><td>Yes</td></tr>
<tr><td>Education/Training:</td><td>Marton Valley School 1988–1993
GCSE
English C   History D
Maths B   Biology C
French A   Geography C

Worsthall CFE 1993–1994
Pitman's Secretarial Course 1
Typing RSA 2
Shorthand 80wpm
Office Practice – Pass
English – Pass</td></tr>
<tr><td>Work Experience:</td><td>Paley's Newsagents, Marton
1993–1994
Shelf stocking/customer service

Au pair, Lyons, 1994–1995
French conversation</td></tr>
<tr><td>Hobbies and Interests:</td><td>Country & Western music
Wok cooking
Tennis</td></tr>
</table>

* If you don't have a licence, simply leave out the line. Only mention those things that reflect your strengths. Equally, if there are other things which show you in a good light, put them in. Each CV is different, there is no set plan, but it should be concise and logically presented.

At the Interview

Interviews make everybody nervous. You cannot help that but you can and should take care to prepare beforehand. Think about your good points, work out your answers to likely questions, find out what you can about the company, pay attention to your appearance, arrive in good time. These are ways of ensuring that, even when panic sets in you will appear like a swan, calm and rational on the surface, even if paddling hard underwater!

If you can do so unobtrusively, take three or four deep, slow breaths before facing the interviewer. It will relax you. When the interviewer asks you to sit down, sit well back, upright and with your hands resting in your lap. Look at him when either of you are speaking and *smile*. It is impossible to be tense while smiling. Here are some points to bear in mind.

Do not be late. Make sure you know where you are going and be there early.

Take care how you look. Dress neatly and conservatively, use minimum make-up and scent, check your hair and nails are clean and tidy, wear clean shoes.

Don't smoke, even if invited to do so and refuse coffee or tea. (You do not know the attitude to smoking in that office and no one can drink and talk.)

Speak up, look up and take your time. People say 'you know', or 'sort of' because they have not thought about what they want to say. It is intensely irritating for the interviewer. So think about your answer before starting to speak. That is where your pre-planning will help.

Do not give Yes and No answers. Tell the interviewer about yourself. Tell him how good you are too, do not be too modest. You are selling yourself, remember.

Do not fight with the interviewer. He may try to upset you to see how you react to pressure. Smile sweetly, put forward your case and then shut up.

Take an interest in the company and the job. Your preparation should include finding out what you can about the company's activities. (Larger companies have a brochure, for instance, so you could ask for one before the interview.)

Never be rude about a previous employer. This is something else to think about before the interview.

Each interview will be different of course but in essence all will cover the same ground. The interviewer will ask about you, as a person: family, school, hobbies and interests. This is mainly to make you relax a bit and talk. Then he will want to know about your work skills and motivation. Why are you applying for this particular job? How do you see your career shaping – what do you hope to be doing in five years' time? He will certainly tell you about the job and the company and then ask you if you have any questions. You may then like to ask about details of what the job actually involves, who you will be working with and for and information about salary, hours of work and company benefits, such as training, canteen and sports facilities.

At the end of the interview, smile, thank the interviewer, say good-bye to his secretary and the receptionist (they may be asked what they thought of you, so leave a good impression). If you are offered the job and do not want it, do not refuse immediately. Ask for time to think it over.

Some further notes
There is a growing tendency to administer 'character' tests, before or after interviews, in addition to any skills tests you may be given. These are usually multiple-choice questions, designed to show whether or not you are a worthy citizen and likely to be good at your job. Some people become quite good at guessing the right answers! I always take the view that if the company do not like my attitude I am unlikely to like theirs either.

Do think of a good reason for wanting the job. 'Because Mum and Dad are fed up with me mooning around the house' may be honest and has been used, but is not what the employer wants to hear. It is a comment made by many employers that applicants fail to show they are enthusiastic. See the *Introduction* about a competitive edge.

Similarly, avoid making a statement, in terms of dress or manner. It may be tedious to conform but, if you are serious about getting a good job, you will have to. The employer will be thinking of how you will fit in with colleagues, how you will appear to customers and of your likely commitment to the company, and your outward appearance is all there is to go on at an interview.

Try to analyse why you did not get any job, in a positive way. You can always ask, although they will not always tell you. It may be you are too diffident (or too cocksure) in your attitude; that you did not do enough background research about the job and company; that you are aiming too high or too low, for your qualifications. Whatever the reason, it is important to discover it before the next interview.

Accepting a Job

Before you get your contract of employment, before you even write a letter of acceptance, you should make sure you know your position. No one should accept a job without understanding what the job entails, what the hours and rate of pay are and what the holiday entitlement is. It is no use saying later that you did not realise what the job involved, or you thought you were entitled to four weeks holiday when it turns out to be two. In practice, an employer will normally write to you, offering the job and setting out these details. So, if you are offered the job at the interview, you can say: 'Yes please, in principle. You will write to me about the details will you?'

Contract of Employment

A contract of employment exists as soon as someone offers you a job (even verbally) at a certain rate of pay and you accept. Within 13 weeks of your starting work the employer is required by law to give you written details of your contract. These cover:

Job title
Pay
How you are paid (weekly, monthly, etc)
Hours of work
Holiday entitlement and pay
Length of notice
Disciplinary and grievance procedures
Pension rights.

If you are not given a copy of your contract within 13 weeks of joining a firm, you should ask for it. The contract of employment is a legal document, so make sure that you keep it in a safe place.

Chapter 5
Employment Agencies

It is one thing to screw up your courage and go for a job interview. For many people, finding a prospective employer in the first place is just as difficult and can be depressing, especially if you are inexperienced and lack the confidence to present yourself well in a letter, on the telephone or through your CV. Fortunately, there is no need for you to go it alone. You can get help from your local Careers Guidance Office, in the first instance, while your local Jobcentre will give you advice and make interview appointments for you. Or you can go and see an employment agent.

Employment agents are paid by companies to find suitable staff for them, so they do not cost you anything. On the other hand, they are always looking for bright, reliable people, without whom they cannot satisfy their customers. So, anyone who has just qualified or decided to look for office work of any kind would do well to start by visiting a few. Until you have actually had some job experience they may well not be able to help you directly, because their clients demand experience. They will be able to offer helpful advice and suggestions however and you will gain valuable practice in projecting yourself, in addition to making contacts which may well prove useful later.

Going to an agency is a bit like going for a job interview, in that you will want to convince the staff in the agency that you are a good prospect; but unlike one in the sense that they will want you to succeed and will be keen to help you. Don't just drop in off the street, be positive about what you are doing and look your best when you go to see them.

A consultant will interview you, to find out about you and what you are looking for, run a few tests to establish what you can do and perhaps help with your CV preparation. If you are not yet ready, she will suggest what you should do to improve your skills and then restart the process. The national agencies quite often offer you a 'job pack' wallet, giving details of all you need to know, for you to take home and study.

If you go to an interview through an agency, the consultant will check with the employer how you got on, obtaining information which may well help in future, even if you do not get that particular job. Employment agencies will also tell you about prospective companies and of course they know all about current rates of pay and employment incentives.

Permanent or Temporary?

You should give some thought to whether you want a permanent job or to work as a temp. We touched on this subject earlier (p. 21). A permanent job gives you a measure of security and a feeling of belonging to an organisation, to say nothing of regular pay cheques and fringe benefits. On the other hand, you have to win the job, often in the face of considerable competition and you do not get to know the company you have joined until you start working there.

As a temp, you have to convince the agency, rather than the company, that you can do the work required and cope with different people, different organisations and different pressures, every week or so. If you can succeed and you like the challenges presented to you, you will earn more money per hour, be able to choose, more or less, when and where you want to work and have an opportunity to find a company where you would like to work permanently. On the other hand, in slack times, there may not always be work for you. One way of getting over that problem is to use more than one agency but you must be careful here, because you also need to be the person the agency telephones first and they will only do that if you are normally available to help them.

Incentives

In busy times, when secretaries are in short supply, some of the larger agencies offer considerable loyalty incentives to their temps. Holidays with pay, regular pay rises, bonuses and holiday prizes are just a few examples of what may be available. Some of them can provide training, especially in the crucial field of office technology, where the ability to learn quickly how to use different types of office equipment can be a great advantage.

Above all, you will quite likely find someone you can talk to and who knows what would suit you – a great comfort in gloomy times.

Addresses

You will find Employment Agents in Yellow Pages. We have included the national agencies here, one or more of which will have a branch near you. They are not necessarily better than local firms, although they are more likely to have useful starter kits, training facilities and other perks to offer, ideal for a beginner.

Alfred Marks Bureau Limited
Adia House
PO Box 311
Borehamwood
Herts WD6 1WD
Tel: 0181 207 5000

Blue Arrow Personnel Services Limited
Blue Arrow House
83 Camp Road
St Albans
Herts AL1 5UA
Tel: 01727 866266

Brook Street
Clarence House
134 Hatfield Road
St Albans
Herts AL1 4JB
Tel: 01727 848292

Manpower Plc
International House
66 Chiltern Street
London W1M 1PR
Tel: 0171 224 6688

Reed Employment
140 The Broadway
Tolworth
Surrey KT6 7JE
Tel: 0181 399 5221

Chapter 6
Office Machines

Word processors and their big brothers, mini and mainframe computers, have removed much of the drudgery from office work, in the same way that washing machines and microwave ovens have helped in the house. At the same time, they have vastly enhanced the work that can be done by a secretary, typist or clerk, by putting in her hands the opportunity for all kinds of creative activity undreamed of ten years ago.

You will hear of desk-top publishing, for instance, even if you are not soon involved in it. This is simply the ability to compose a document of any length, complete with graphs, charts and diagrammatic illustrations; to set it up correctly on the page, using different headings, typescripts and other printing devices, and variation or emphasis to create the right effect, free of errors and then to print as many copies as required. The effect is magical and yet mastery of the technique is open to anyone who can learn to type.

In another field, you might use what are known as spread-sheets and computer programs which deal with numbers of any sort, prices, sales figures, accounts, etc. You can do all kinds of complicated calculations, without a qualified accountant, simply by spending a day or two learning what to ask or to tell the computer. The most exciting question is always 'What if...?', by which you might, for instance, ask the computer to calculate what would happen to profits if all the prices were raised by so much, or half the company's branches were to close!

There are many college courses you can take to prepare you for using word processors. Once you have the basic understanding needed, most companies provide training at work to familiarise you with the actual machines and procedures they employ. As noted in the previous chapter, some employment agencies also provide both initial and 'switch' training on different software packages. The basis of all your training should still be typing, with or without shorthand. This is because an ability to type is the first requirement for operating any sort of keyboard machine, except the simpler data-entry machines, and also because there are still some offices which use electronic typewriters.

Computers carry out both complex and routine data-processing functions, such as payroll calculations, invoicing and product costing, in a fraction of the time and with none of the drudgery involved in doing the same things manually. Some have an electronic mailing function (email), by which messages can be passed to other computers in an organisation or outside, by telephone, saving two days in the post.

VDU Work or Data Entry. VDU stands for visual display unit. The operator has a screen and keyboard, linked to a central computer, through which she can seek information about stock levels, invoices, etc, or insert such information. So a shop assistant using a VDU can find out the part number of an item, whether it is in stock, its price and any discount information, raise an invoice if she sells it, and at the same time automatically alter the stock figures. This machine is so easy to use you do not even need to be able to type to operate it.

Word Processors, instead of typewriters, are the machines now mainly used by secretaries. They consist of a screen, on which the typed matter appears; a keyboard, like a typewriter but with additional keys for the computer functions, and a printer, which produces the finished document when the typist is satisfied with it. The WP can also carry out computer functions such as spreadsheets and can be linked into an electronic mailing system. It retains the documents you have made on hard or floppy disks, which are often built into the WP and also provide a highly efficient filing system, although you are advised always to make a paper copy of anything precious, in case the disk is wiped clean, damaged or destroyed by accident.

A word processor is just one form of **Personal Computer** (PC), so called because it is designed to be used by a single operating clerk or typist/secretary. Not only have WPs considerably reduced the need for cumbersome filing systems or card indices, it is also possible to update a routine document or send out a bulk mailing by simply amending the necessary file, without lengthy retyping. Items can be added, altered, deleted or assembled at the touch of a button. Any kind of information stored can be converted into reports or lists and printed as desired. Selected customer lists can be merged with selected product or service information to produce individually addressed letters and envelopes for a mailing.

By using the appropriate instruction software, these machines can carry out all the functions required of an accounts office. Instead of being primarily used for writing (dedicated word processor), they can be used to carry out complicated calculations, as computers. The simple word processor on which these words have been typed is quite happy producing a cash flow spreadsheet, doing all the sums automatically, or running off sticky addressed labels for a customer mailing, as well as a hundred and one other things. It is just a matter of feeding it the correct software.

Double-Sided and Self-Collating Copiers. Automatic copiers, capable of printing over 50 copies a minute, are now a normal part of office life. In addition, these machines can also do double-sided copying, photo-reduce, overlay and collate copies of documents for you, which takes the drudgery away from photocopying. Some models can copy in colour.

Fax (Facsimile) Machines. Fax machines transmit copies of documents, including illustrations, by telephone, anywhere in the world, provided the other party has a fax machine. The advantages over a telephone call are that you have a record of what was sent and that you can demonstrate exactly what you wish. In the case of a diagram, for instance, the recipient can make alterations to his drawing and fax it back to you. Both parties now know exactly what is required and it has taken the minimum amount of time to achieve this, without risk of damage to, or loss in the post of, the original, to say nothing of the time factor. You can learn to use a fax machine in about five minutes.

Electronic Typewriters. There are still offices which use typewriters instead of word processors. Electronic typewriters are highly sophisticated machines. They are self-correcting, allowing the production of perfect copies. They have memories, from which stored documents can be re-used or revised. You can instruct the machine to search for and replace words, lines or paragraphs in the text, or automatically to print a standard letter addressed to different people. Some can have a screen added, like a WP screen, allowing editing of a complete document before printing it. In fact, these machines do many of the things a word processor can do, so they are the next best thing.

Even where electronic machines are not generally used, it is quite usual to find at least one in use alongside the WPs. This is because they are ideal for quick little jobs, like envelopes, or even labels, memos and notes. The WP can do these jobs but has to be set up for them, by which time they can be done on a typewriter.

Part 2

Chapter 7
Qualifications and Courses Available

Over the next 50 or so pages are set out the main certificating bodies for courses and qualifications in the field of business.

At first glance the information may seem to be a blur and, indeed, it is not meant to be read like a book. Here are ideas for jobs; suggestions as to how you might start to plan your career; skills, or 'competences', as they are now called, which you should consider working to achieve, or which may excite or interest you.

While many of the courses run by the different organisations are similar, all have their individual approach and it is the essence of these differences that I have tried to capture. So skim, dip in, allow your eye to be caught by a word or phrase and then investigate further.

National Council for Vocational Qualifications
222 Euston Road, London NW1 2BZ; 0171 387 9898 (Publications: 0171 728 1893)

The NCVQ is the body responsible for developing and administering NVQs, which are awarded by such as BTEC, RSA, etc (see below), either directly, or through a school or college. The NCVQ has produced two complementary programmes: General National Vocational Qualifications (GNVQs), which are intended primarily for 16–18 year-olds in full-time education; and NVQs, which are more specialised in content, primarily for adult education. Neither programme is exclusive to these groups. Students may take GNVQs and NVQs, GCSE or GCE A- and AS-level subjects at the same time and may study full-time or part-time, as they wish. The idea is to make learning as flexible and relevant to individual requirements as possible.

NVQs are available at five levels, based on degrees of competence, from ability to deal with routine and predictable problems, at level 1, roughly equivalent to GCSE, to senior management, postgraduate attainments at level 5.

GNVQs are on three levels: Foundation, Intermediate and Advanced. Their equivalent to other certificates is like this:

GNVQ level	Description	Broadly equivalent to
1	Foundation	4 GCSEs at Grade D or below
2	Intermediate	4+ GCSEs at Grades A to C
3	Advanced	2 GCE A levels

Levels 1 and 2 are normally one year, full-time courses, while level 3 is a two-year, full-time course.

National Vocational Qualifications (NVQs)

In the last few years there has been a major shift in training emphasis, throughout the UK, from formal examination to vocational qualification, based specifically on the skills, knowledge and understanding employers need. National Vocational Qualifications (NVQs) and Scottish Vocational Qualifications (SVQs) have advanced from being new, interesting, even exciting ideas, to being the norm. The major examining bodies, BTEC, LCCI, PEI, RSA, etc have all completely revised their programmes to encompass NVQ requirements. Colleges of Further Education and the like are now increasingly only offering NVQ-based study in the area of career training.

For those who find formal examinations a terrifying and frequently catastrophic experience, NVQs offer an altogether more satisfactory way of allowing your talents to flower, while those with strings of GCSE and GCE A and AS level awards will find a new challenge in the practical experience of work-centred study.

NVQs are based on national standards, reflecting workplace requirements. Students are assessed in work conditions and NVQs are guarantees of competence. Study can be at work, school, college or home and NVQs are in unit form.

Unit-based systems are good news, because they ensure that you can study what interests you, within a broad framework of choice. Typically, an NVQ will have mandatory units, which a student must pass, plus optional units, from a wide range.

For instance, anyone wanting to be a secretary must be able to type, a mandatory skill, but can select audio, copy or shorthand typing as a preferred option. Or you might be very much better at typing than the NVQ demands but not at other subjects required. In that case you can gain a higher unit *and receive credit for it* within the NVQ. Examples of some of the available units from the various examining bodies are given below. Suffice to say here that the system has literally something for everyone.

GNVQs are designed primarily for young people in full-time education who want to keep their career options open. They are meant to prepare people for a range of related occupations, or for higher education.

Foundation level GNVQs comprise six vocational units, three of which can be from different vocational areas, plus three 'core skill' units, common to all GNVQs: application of number; communication; and information technology.

Intermediate level GNVQs typically comprise: four mandatory units, based on the requirements of the course; two optional units, which can be on completely different subjects; and three core skill units.

Similarly, Advanced GNVQs might have three mandatory units, four optional units and the three core skills.

GNVQs are designed to fit you for work or prepare you for further study, or indeed both. They keep your options open. Good work can, on completion of the course, lead to a 'merit' or 'distinction' grade assessment.

The flexibility of the NVQ system is illustrated by NCVQ as pulling down the barriers to achievement, thus:

Old system	*NVQs*
Can I do that qualification?	
No, you haven't got the right entry qualifications.	Yes, there are no barriers to entry.
I want to get qualified but I work full time. Can I do both?	
No, you've got to go to college for two years.	Yes, you can do some units at work and some in your own time.
I've got 20 years' experience. Will that count for anything?	
No, I'm afraid you'll have to do the course.	Yes, you can get credit for your competence.

Can I just do the bit of the qualification that relates to my work?

No, it's the whole qualification or nothing.

Yes, you can select the units you want to work towards and we can work out a programme for you.

National Database

The National Database of Vocational Qualifications contains all the NVQs and the units required to attain them and how these units are made up. So you can plan your own training according to your particular needs. Your local college, Careers Guidance Office or Training and Enterprise Council will tell you where the nearest access point is.

The National Record of Achievement

The NRA is a portable summary of an individual's training progress. It contains several elements: brief personal details; a summary of qualifications and credits; a summary of other achievements and experiences; a personal statement by the individual.

In addition it contains a school-leaver's achievements within the school curriculum and for adults an employment history. In other words, the NRA is an official CV.

'As a summary document it is the end product of a process of assessing, reviewing and recording achievement. The NRA encourages the individual to take pride in past achievements and plan future development.' (*NCVQ*)

Training Credits

People on Training Credits work for NVQs at Level 2 and above.

Training Credits are open to anyone who has left school, whether working or not and are guaranteed to 16 and 17 year-olds who have not yet found work.

If the trainee is employed, full wages are paid. If not, a minimum payment of £40 per week at 16 is made for the duration of the training, plus certain travel allowances.

Training Credits enable people to qualify for the work they want to do. Programmes are tailored to be of an appropriate length (eg, one or two years) to suit individuals. Learning is by the most suitable method: on the job, college, open learning.

Training Credits are run by Training and Enterprise Councils (TECs), or Local Enterprise Councils (LECs) in Scotland. Your careers teacher, Careers Guidance Office, Jobcentre or Citizens Advice Bureau will be able to tell you how to find your local TEC. They are run by prominent local business people and arrange on-the-job training and work experience. There are 81 TECs, nationwide.

Getting help. It can sometimes be difficult to find the various agencies who can help you. You will probably not find your local TEC under that heading. For instance, the Oxford TEC is called Heart of England Training and Enterprise Council. The Careers Guidance Office will not be under 'Careers' except as a sub-heading under your local or county Council. For Jobcentre, try Employment Service or Employment Department, and so on. It is all to test your initiative! Do persevere, however. They are generally very helpful people who are easy to talk to.

Royal Society of Arts (RSA)
Westwood Way, Coventry CV4 8HS; 01203 470033
RSA schemes are widely available at schools, colleges of all kinds, and from employers and training agencies. Indeed, they claim that around 8,000 centres, worldwide, run RSA courses.

Series Examinations
The single-subject examinations are intended, primarily, for students on clerical, secretarial and business courses in schools and colleges. They are suitable both for those on vocational courses and for those requiring a background knowledge of the world of business.

Examinations are available in three stages. Stage I indicates a student has the knowledge or skills to begin employment, Stage II shows sound understanding and competence, and Stage III indicates a high degree of proficiency.

Text Processing
Audio-Transcription Stages I, II and III

Core Text Processing Skills

Medical Audio-Transcription* Stage II

Shorthand Transcription Stages II and III

Typewriting Skills Stages I, II and III

Typewriting Skills* (French) and (German) Stage I

Word Processing Stages I, II and III

Word Processing (Audio) Stage I

Word Processing* (French) and (German) Stage I

* Pilot scheme

Text Processing Modular Awards
A new series, to reflect the level required for NVQ Administration, is currently under development. A new Diploma is being introduced at Stages II and III, to recognise all-round achievement in Text Processing.
Text Processing Part 1, Stages I, II and III
Audio-Transcription Part 2, Stages I, II and III
Shorthand-Transcription Part 2, Stages I, II and III
Typewriting Part 2, Stages I, II and III
Word Processing Part 2, Stages I, II and III
Medical Audio-Transcription Part 2, Stage II
Medical Word Processing Part 2, Stage II

Information Technology
(In addition to these Series Examinations, see IT Qualifications, below.)
Spreadsheets, Stage II
Databases, Stage II
Desktop Publishing, Stage II

English & Communications
(See also Language Qualifications, below.)
Communication in Business, Stage I and II
English Language, Stages I, II and III
Communicative English Skills: reading, writing, receptive and interactive.

Accounting, Bookkeeping & Business
Accounting, Stages I and II
Background to Business, Stages I and II
Bookkeeping, Stage I
Numeracy, Stage I and II
Practical Bookkeeping, Stages II and III

Skills Tests

Computer Keyboard Skills	Spell-test (Business)*
Copy-typing Speed	Spell-test (General)*
Medical Shorthand Speed	Word Processing Functions
Shorthand*	

* Pilot scheme

IT Examinations
Computer Literacy and Information Technology (CLAIT) Stage I
Profile Certificate
Application of Office Technology, Stage II

GCSE Cross-Qualification Schemes
Information Studies
Information Systems
National Curriculum Information Technology

National Vocational Qualifications
These schemes are competence based. Their flexible design means
that they:

- can be work or college based
- are designed for easy movement between schemes
- incorporate communication, numerical and information technology skills, plus some aspects of personal effectiveness
- are aligned with National Council for Vocational Qualifications schemes.

Information Technology

Using Information Technology
Level 1, for those performing routine functions, under
instruction.
Level 2, for those performing complex tasks on their own
responsibility.

Controlling Use of Information Technology
Level 3, for those taking control of their own area of responsibility,
including supervising others.

Administration

Administration, Level 1
Nine units, including: health and safety; producing text; processing information; handling mail; operating and taking care of
equipment; stock control; effectiveness of working relationships;
efficiency of workflow.

Administration, Level 2
Nine units, including: self-development; health and safety; creat-

ing effective working relationships; preparing documents; effectiveness of workflow; data control; handling information.

Administration, Level 3
Ten units, from 21 elements of competence, plus an optional unit and a shorthand transcription element. This is for progression from Level 2; working students wishing for a national certificate; full-time or part-time students; 'returners' requiring recognition of previous achievements.
(New NVQs, at Levels 3 and 4, are in preparation. Check on availability.)

Legal Units for Administration
Five additional units are available to add to Administration NVQs: property transactions; litigation; processing payment; private client; corporate services.

NVQ/GNVQ Language Units
For listening, speaking, reading and writing in French, German, Italian and Spanish.

Other Verified Schemes, Including Profile Schemes

Bilingual Business Administration (English/Welsh) Level 1 and Level 2 (Administrative, Financial and Secretarial) and Level 3, Administration
The bilingual qualifications follow the format of English NVQs in the same subject, except that candidates will need to be equally competent in English and Welsh.

Diploma in Information Technology
For those already competent in basic skills who are qualified to work on their own in organisations where office-automated systems are used for most areas of work.

Advanced Diploma in Information Technology
For those employed at a senior level, with some responsibility for other staff, in a fully-automated, information-handling and communications environment.

Higher Diploma in Administrative and Secretarial Procedures
Higher Diploma in Administrative Procedures
Higher Bilingual Diploma in Administrative and Secretarial Procedures (Welsh/English) (Pilot)
For those in employment or on a course involving a broad range of administrative and organisational tasks of a complex and specialised nature, involving planning and problem solving and a significant degree of personal accountability.

Vocational Certificate (Information Technology)
For anyone working or proposing to work as a junior clerk in an office where most information is handled using technology. The course includes communication, numeracy, use of text processing facilities, computerised office procedures and electronic mail.

Practical Skills Profile
For those requiring accreditation of their skills in: communication; numeracy; information technology; problem solving; personal effectiveness. This is not a course.

Enterprise Skills Profile
For those involved in Training Credits, community/voluntary schemes who wish to gain recognition of enterprise skills. Covers a range including: communication; personal effectiveness; problem solving; numeracy; information technology. It is not a course.

GNVQs (see page 45)

Foundation Business
The mandatory units are: processing business payments; investigating business and customers; and investigating working in business.
    The six options, of which candidates choose three, are: contributing to a team activity; health and safety; scheduling and booking; processing business information; providing office support; investigating employment.

Intermediate Business
The four mandatory units are: business organisations and employment; people in business organisations; financial transactions; consumers and customers.
    The four options (choose two) are: business communication;

promotion and sales; business in Europe; and enterprise activities.

Advanced Business
The eight mandatory units are: business in the economy; business systems; marketing; human resources; employment in the market economy; financial transactions and monitoring; financial resources; business planning.

The nine options (choose four) are: quality; safety and the environment; business law; financial services; leadership and teamwork; business and the European Union; business practice; customer service; two language units (French/German/Italian/Spanish).

Foundation Information Technology (IT) (Pilot)
The three mandatory units are: using information technology; the use and impact of IT systems; investigating working in IT.

The options (choose three) are: contributing to a team activity; document production; graphic design; measurement and control systems; obtaining information from electronic sources; information collecting and processing.

Intermediate Information Technology (Pilot)
The four mandatory units are: organisation and the application of IT; people and IT; developing information processing systems; using IT.

Options (choose two) are: electronic communications systems; graphic design; operating on IT systems; introduction to programming.

Advanced Information Technology (Pilot)
The eight mandatory units are: data handling; measurement and control systems and modelling; communications and networking; software and software installations and customisation; systems analysis; data modelling and database structures; individuals, society and IT; IT projects and teamwork.

The options (choose four) are: relational databases; program design and methodologies; programming languages and techniques; programming; system design; mathematical applications for IT; business applications of IT; multimedia systems.

Language Examinations

Certificate in Business Language Competence (Basic)
For those who wish to demonstrate basic communicative skills in French, German, Italian or Spanish.

Certificate in Business Language Competence (Survival)
For those wishing for a limited repertoire of language structures and vocabulary, within routine and practical business contexts (French, German, Italian, Spanish).

Certificate in Business Language Competence (Threshold)
For those wishing to use a limited structure and vocabulary, within familiar business contexts. Six elements: listening; reading; doing business by telephone; exchanging opinions; conversing formally; writing in a target language.

Certificate in Business Language Competence (Operational)
For those using a range of language structures and vocabulary, within a variety of business contexts. Six elements: listening; reading; doing business by telephone; exchanging opinions; delivering prepared presentations; writing in a target language.

Certificate in Business Language Competence (Advanced)
For those using a broad range of language structures and vocabulary, within a wide variety of business contexts. Five elements: listening; reading; discussing products and services; delivering prepared presentations; writing.

London Chamber of Commerce and Industry
Marlowe House, Station Road, Sidcup, Kent DA15 7BJ; 0181 302 0261

The LCCI is one of the oldest and largest examining bodies in the business field and is internationally recognised. Their Group Secretarial qualifications and Information Technology Awards are designed to test up-to-date skills and problem-solving techniques, from GCSE equivalent to senior management level.

The list of colleges offering LCCI courses is not exhaustive. It is the latest available, but it is worthwhile applying to your local college, even if it is not listed, or contacting the LCCI directly.

Group Secretarial Awards
You can qualify for a full award, or pass each component separately. Compulsory components may later be converted to a full award, provided that all are passed within three years from the original start.

Secretarial Studies Certificate
For those acting as, or seeking to be, secretaries to junior or middle management. The compulsory components are equivalent to GCSE grades A–C and are: communication; transcription; office procedures; background to business, plus project.

Options are: word processing; practical word processing, first level; practical computing; shorthand 70/80 wpm.

Private Secretary's Certificate
For those acting as, or seeking to be, a private secretary or assistant to middle or senior management. The compulsory components, equivalent to GCE A level, are: communication; transcription; office organisation and secretarial procedures; structure of business.

The options are: information processing; practical word processing, second level; shorthand 90/100 wpm.

Private and Executive Secretary's Diploma
This graduate or postgraduate level Diploma is designed to evaluate the business, technical, secretarial and communication skills of someone working as or wishing to be a secretary/PA at top management level. Compulsory components are: communication; meetings; transcription (shorthand or audio); secretarial administration; management appreciation.

The options are: information processing; text processing.

First Certificate for Legal Secretaries
For those acting, or seeking to act, as a secretary in a legal office. The compulsory components are equivalent to GCSE grades A–C, and are: communication; transcription; business and administration, Level 2, plus project; law and its terminology.

Options are: word processing, plus portfolio; practical word processing, Level 1; practical computing; shorthand 70/80 wpm.

Second Certificate for Legal Secretaries
For those acting, or seeking to act, as a senior secretary in a legal office. The compulsory components, equivalent to GCE A level,

are: communication; transcription; business administration, Level 3; law and its terminology, Level 3.

Options are: information processing, plus portfolio; practical word processing, Level 2; shorthand 90/100 wpm.

Secretarial Skills
Audio-Transcription: Level 1, 25 wpm; Level 2, 35 wpm; Level 3, 45 wpm.

Office Procedures (Levels 1 and 2). How an office works and the various support services it needs.

Shorthand (Levels 1, 2 and 3) at speeds from 50 wpm to 140 wpm.

Typewriting: Level 1, 25 wpm; Level 2, 35 wpm; Level 3, 45 wpm.

Other available secretarial awards include:
Diploma in European Business Administration.
European Executive Assistant Certificate.
Commercial Language Assistant Certificate.

Information Technology (IT)

Practical Word Processing, Level 1
Six assignments, ranging from opening files to formatting and layout of documents.

Practical Word Processing, Level 2
Six assignments, as for Level 1, plus additional functions ranging from form design to file management.

Text Processing, Level 3 (Practical)
As for Level 2, plus a range of advanced functions involved in text processing. Keyboard competence essential for candidates.

Word Processing, Level 2
A practical assessment of knowledge and use of technology in the modern office.

Practical Computing, Level 1
Practical assessment of competence in at least two of the following: computerised accounting; computerised graphics; database; spreadsheets; videotex; word processing.

Elements of Data Processing, Level 1
Written, plus practical, assessment of competence in at least two applications packages. Syllabus covers data storage; computer networks; the Data Protection Act 1984; health and safety.

Information Processing, Level 3
Information processing and related technology in the modern office, including types of system, information processing operations and applications and developments in the modern office.

Business Information Systems, Level 3
The business and financial aspects of computer applications. The economic importance of computer-based information systems. The syllabus covers: systems analysis and design; data processing; programs; software and application packages; contemporary computer equipment.

Group Awards
The following group awards in IT are also available:
Group Diploma in Data Processing, Level 3
Information Processing Group Certificate, Level 3
Word Processing Group Certificate, Level 2.

Colleges in the United Kingdom
The courses offered are coded as follows:

Private and Executive Secretary's Diploma (D)
Private Secretary's Certificate (C)
Second Certificate for Legal Secretaries (L)
Secretarial Studies Certificate (S)
First Certificate for Legal Secretaries (l)
*Word/information processing

C		**Amersham**, Amersham and Wycombe College
C	D	*__Armagh__, Armagh College of Further Education
C		*__Banbridge__, Banbridge College of Further Education
C		**Banbury**, North Oxfordshire College
S		**Bedford**, Hastingsbury School
C	D	*__Belfast__, Belfast Institute of Further and Higher Education

S	l	C	L	D	
S		C			***Bexley**, Bexley College
	l				***Birmingham**, Bournville College of Further Education
				D	***Blackpool**, Blackpool & The Fylde College of Further and Higher Education
				D	***Bracknell**, Bracknell College
				D	***Bradford**, Bradford and Ilkley Community College
S		C			**Bridgwater**, Bridgwater College
S					**Bromley**, Hayes School
S		C			**Coalville**, Coalville Technical College
				D	**Chichester**, Chichester College of Arts, Science & Technology
	l			D	**Coventry**, Coventry Technical College
		C			**Downpatrick**, Down College of Further Education
		C			**Dungannon**, East Tyrone College of Further Education
		C		D	***Eastleigh**, Eastleigh College of Further Education
				D	***Exeter**, Keystrokes Secretarial College
S		C		D	**Farnborough**, Farnborough College of Technology
		C			**Grimsby**, Grimsby College of Technology
S		C		D	***Haverfordwest**, Pembrokeshire College
		C			***Heanor**, South East Derbyshire College
		C		D	**Hereford**, Herefordshire Technical College
		C		D	***Huddersfield**, Huddersfield Technical College
S					**Ilford**, Canon Palmer RC School
S					**Ipswich**, Suffolk College of Higher and Further Education
				D	***Kettering**, Tresham Institute
S		C		D	**Kidderminster**, Kidderminster College of Further Education
		C			**Lincoln**, North Lincolnshire College
		C			**Loughborough**, Loughborough Technical College
				D	***Middlesbrough**, Kirby College of Further Education
		C	L		***Norwich**, Norwich City College
S		C			***Nottingham**, Basford Hall College of Further Education
				D	**Preston**, Preston College
				D	**Redruth**, Cornwall College
		C		D	**Richmond**, Surrey, Kudos Training

l	L		**Rochester**, Mid-Kent College of Higher and Further Education
S			**Romford**, Frances Bardsley School
l	L		**Romford**, Barking College of Technology
S			**Romford**, Chadwell Heath High School
S			**Romford**, Redbridge College of Further Education
	C		**Rotherham**, Rotherham College of Arts & Technology
		D	*St Helens, Community College
S	C		**Salisbury**, La Retraite Convent School
	C		**Scarborough**, Yorkshire Coast College of Further and Higher Education
S	C	D	**Southampton**, Colesway College
	C		**Southend**, The SE Essex College of Art and Technology
	C		*Stamford, Stamford College
	C		**Stourbridge**, Stourbridge College
S	C	D	*Sutton Coldfield, Sutton Coldfield College of Further Education
l	C L		*Swansea, Swansea College
	C L		**Swansea**, Institute of Higher Education
S	C		**Truro**, Truro College
		D	*Twickenham, West London Institute of Higher Education
		D	**Wigan**, Wigan College of Technology
	C		**Wirral**, County Grammar School for Girls
	C		**Wirral**, Wirral Metropolitan College
		D	*Wolverhampton, Wulfrun College of Further Education

London Postal Districts

S	C	D	*London College of Higher Education, SW4
	C	D	Queen's Secretarial College, SW7

City & Guilds of London Institute (C & G)
1 Giltspur Street, London EC1A 9DD; 0171 294 2468

C & G was founded in 1878, by the City of London and certain Livery Companies. Its awards span seven levels, from Foundation to Fellowship of City & Guilds of London Institute, and include an annual Prince Philip Medal and Gold, Silver and Bronze awards for outstanding achievement. All C & G awards offer an employment-based route to professional qualifications.

While C & G are not primarily concerned with office and

secretarial awards, their Pitman's Division concentrates on these areas (see below); they do run GNVQs and NVQs in Administration and Information Technology and Customer Service, which are worth considering, particularly if they are preferred by your school or college of choice. C & G note that Ford, Sainsbury's and the Bank of England are among the organisations using their schemes for in-house training.

NVQ in Information Technology
C & G NVQs in IT are at four levels and concentrate on computer operation, as opposed to word processing. Thus, the units at Level 1 are: stand-alone computer operation; network computer operation; central computer services operation; using IT.

Level 2 develops the above skills, plus: software production and delivery and selection; installation and support of stand-alone systems.

Level 3 covers supervision of Level 1 and 2 units, plus multi-user systems and various units connected with design and installation of information systems.

Level 4 is a Computer Systems Management level.

NVQ in Customer Service, Level 3
This NVQ represents an alternative career route for you to consider. C & G notes that HMSO, Sainsbury's, W H Smith, a health authority and a college of further education (students are also customers) are among those implementing this NVQ, all recognising the crucial importance of their customers.

Units include: maintain reliable customer service; communicate with customers; develop positive working relationships with customers; initiate and evaluate change to improve service to customers.

Pitman Examinations Institute (PEI)
1 Giltspur Street, London EC1A 9DD; 0171 294 2468

PEI is a Division of the City & Guilds of London Institute. It tests office, secretarial and business skills, including information technology, numeracy and accounts. It also specialises in languages, including English for vocational and specific purposes, for those using it as either a first or second language at home.

Business Administration

Basic Business Skills Certificate
This is an access route to Administration NVQ, Level 1, for those who wish to work in administrative, secretarial, business and commercial occupations. The scheme is based on continuous appraisal of performance, at a learning centre or in the workplace.

The six units of competence required can be taken (or credited) singly or in a group. Three of the optional units are full unit credits for NVQ Level 1.

The mandatory units are: contribute to the efficiency of the workflow; contribute to the health and safety of the workplace; operate equipment; develop effective working relationships. The optional units (take any two) are: process information; store and retrieve information using an established storage system; produce text following instructions; handle mail.

Administration NVQ, Level 1
There are nine units, to be taken singly or grouped to form a full NVQ.

Administration NVQ, Level 2
Made up of eight mandatory and one or more optional units, to be taken singly or grouped to form a full NVQ.

Administration NVQ, Level 3
This scheme meets the standards required for those wishing to become secretaries or administrative assistants, or to receive skills recognition in these areas.

The ten units of Level 3 focus on problem-solving, decision-making, personal effectiveness, and development of communications skills. Qualification can lead to higher-level education or career advancement.

Office Procedures, Level 1
For office workers, the scheme covers such subjects as: content of office work; staff required and health and safety; effective communications; filing systems; using office machinery.

Office Procedures, Level 2
In addition to the knowledge required at Level 1, the course tests

a broad range of skills and responsibilities associated with office and secretarial procedures.

Administration and Secretarial Procedures, Level 3
For those who are in, or who are preparing for, senior secretarial/ personal assistant or administrative positions. Emphasis is placed on problem-solving, decision-making and awareness of current developments in equipment, systems and technology.

Business Studies, Levels 1 and 2
Level 1 is ideal for those aspiring to secretarial and clerical positions. It covers a general understanding of the principles, organisation, human resources, influences and controls in business.

Level 2, for administrative and managerial roles, looks at business problems and their solutions, in organisation, decision-making, planning and control, resourcing and external and internal influences.

Numeracy and Accounting

Accounting NVQ, Level 2
For those employed, or wishing to work, in business. In addition to four units in common with Administration NVQ Level 2, this scheme has five units in general accounting procedures. Subjects include: keeping petty cash and receipt and payment records; banking; credit documents for services received and supplied; working a payroll system; using a computer; accounting communications.

Commercial Numeracy, Levels 1 and 2
Level 1, for those with no arithmetic/numeracy qualification, seeks to establish a foundation for future development. It tests an individual's ability to apply, calculate and use numerical skills, particularly in business applications.

Level 2, for those wishing to develop further than Level 1, tests ability to calculate, analyse and explain, using numerical skills such as the four rules of arithmetic, ratios, averages and percentages, measure, reading scale drawings and using reference books and tables.

Bookkeeping and Accounts, Levels 1 and 2
Level 1 would qualify you for a junior role in an accounts office.

It provides understanding of bookkeeping and accounts within a business/secretarial studies foundation course.

Level 2 would qualify you for a wide range of routine functions in an accounts office, or acts as a foundation for specialisation study in business and finance. It covers double-entry bookkeeping, control statements, checking accounts records and understanding of financial information about the state of a business.

Accounting, Levels 3 and 4
Level 3 provides a certificate of accounting competence at technician level, for immediate vocational need. It is also for those seeking to become Section Leader or Senior Bookkeeper, or to act as Secretary to a club or voluntary society. It could serve as a basis for further study in Cost and Management Accounting. It assumes knowledge to Bookkeeping and Accounts Level 2 standard.

Level 4 is for those seeking a career in accountancy, or to be Team Leaders, Section Heads or Assistant Accountants in a commercial organisation.

Cost and Management Accounting
Computerised Accounts
PEI also offers courses in Cost and Management Accounting at Level 3, for those wishing to specialise in these areas, as well as in Computerised Accounts, Levels 1 and 2, as a complement to Bookkeeping and Accounts, Levels 1 and 2, understanding of which is a necessary prerequisite.

Typewriting and Shorthand

Typewriting Examinations
Available at Elementary, Intermediate and Advanced Levels, for general office work, junior secretarial and senior secretarial work respectively, these examinations test speed, accuracy and presentation. Included are: typing and display of letters; manuscripts; memoranda; altered typescripts; forms; display material; statistical tabulations; lists; invoices; statements; reports; committee documents.

Typewriting – Profile Speed
A five-minute test, preceded by one-minute reading time, on typewriter or computer keyboard, and including every character on a standard keyboard. The passage uses English of average difficulty and of a business or social nature. Sufficient material is

provided for 100 wpm for five minutes (2,500 finger operations!). You get a certificate, provided you keep within a 2 per cent error tolerance, to the nearest word per minute.

Audio-Transcription

There are three levels of dictation speed: Intermediate 80; Intermediate 100 and Advanced 120 wpm. Dictation is of business letters, or business letter and memorandum, a staff notice or a short business report. Any keyboard can be used. Transcription time is 28 minutes at Intermediate 80 – 17 wpm, 30 minutes at 100 – 20 wpm and 33 minutes at Advanced 120 – 22 wpm.

Shorthand Theory

Transcription into 'New Era' or 'Pitman 2000', as applicable, of longhand, without dictation. Tests are of selected words and simple sentences, to be transcribed into shorthand.

Shorthand Speed

Examinations, of any system, at speeds from 50 wpm to over 200 wpm, as well as accuracy of transcription. Can be live or prerecorded dictation. If the transcription (per typewriter or word processor) is of mailable quality, this is endorsed on the certificate.

Medical Shorthand

Three-minute passages of dictation to test speed of medical note-taking, from 80 wpm to 120 wpm.

Shorthand Transcription

Designed to test ability, at intermediate shorthand speeds of 80 and 100 wpm, to write shorthand, transcribe it accurately and demonstrate keyboarding skills in display and accuracy.

Office Technology and Information Processing

PEI runs a series of examinations to measure the skills and knowledge required by office workers in using hi-tech equipment. They are suitable for those seeking careers in office work, for those seeking advancement and for returners requiring to demonstrate they are up to date.

Aimed at students training to be keyboard operators, rather than typists, but suitable for anyone wishing to develop fast, accurate control of the keyboard. Tests ability to operate an alpha-numeric keyboard efficiently and to proof-read continuous copy.

Text Production Skills
A step on the road to competence in typing and word processing, this examination also introduces the skills required to gain an NVQ Level 1 unit in keyboarding. It demonstrates ability to produce a simple text by using a word processor or typewriter. Also available in French, German and Spanish.

Practical Word Processing, Elementary Level
Particularly suitable for experienced typists or students wishing to demonstrate competence in the use of a word processor, in addition to an ordinary typewriter.

Word Processing, Elementary Level
First-level keyboard skills: handling documents; storage and retrieval; document assembly; editing; proof-reading; merging of text and dates; printing; housekeeping; system maintenance.

Word Processing, Intermediate Level
Preparation, processing and presenting business documents with speed and accuracy. For those seeking employment as a word-processor operator.

Word Processing, Advanced Level
For an operator capable of using the full range of word processing functions, working without supervision.

Masterclass Word Processing
Examines operating skills at the highest level, in terms of applied functions, accuracy, layout and presentation and production rate. For supervisory or senior secretarial staff, or students who have already demonstrated a high level of proficiency at Advanced Level.

Practical Data Processing, Elementary and
Intermediate Levels
Ability to create and manipulate a simple database file. At Elementary Level, for those seeking a first qualification in the practical use of database software. At Intermediate Level, suitable for those seeking to widen their competence.

Practical Spreadsheet Processing, Elementary and
Intermediate Levels
Elementary Level requires ability to use a spreadsheet file. At
Intermediate Level, a file for business application must be created
and maintained.

Understanding Computers
Suitable for those following introductory vocational courses in
computing, or as part of a business or secretarial-studies course.
Demonstrates knowledge in reading a flowchart, interpreting a
passage from a computer magazine, reading and writing short
BASIC routines and in discussing computer applications.

Disk Management
Suitable for those on a foundation course in business studies/
information technology, who also have knowledge and experience of disk management and systems specifications in word
processing, spreadsheets and data processing.

Desktop Publishing, Levels 1 and 2
Level 1: effective application of software package; import text and
graphics and follow precise instructions and measurements.
 Level 2: production of multi-page, multi-column documents,
using imported text and graphics. Understand typesetting con-
ventions. Use software in a systematic and professional manner.

English for Vocational Purposes
'A good standard of English is an important requirement for most
jobs,' PEI notes.

English, Elementary and Intermediate Levels
For those English speakers who have had a disrupted education
and who need to improve their communications skills. Specific
tests in grammar and punctuation are common in both levels.

English for Business Communications, Levels 1, 2 and 3
Level 1: straightforward business communications in English.
 Levels 2 and 3: ability to carry out a series of written tasks
concisely, clearly and accurately.
 All three levels are designed for those who are preparing for, or
who already work in, any occupation requiring the ability to write
business communications in English.

English for Office Skills, Levels 1 and 2
Accuracy in the use and transcription of English and the ability
to perform office-related tasks in accordance with spoken and
written instructions.

English for Speakers of Other Languages
A five-level series for those whose first or main language is not
English. A pass at Advanced Level (5) is set at a standard accepted
by institutions of higher education in the UK as adequate for study
on their courses.

At each level, candidates will be required to show proficiency
appropriate to that level in: reading, writing, listening and
grammar.

Communication in Technical English
This scheme tests understanding of written English of a technical
nature: interpretation of graphical and pictorial information;
ability to write English effectively; ability to produce or complete
various charts from given information.

Business & Technology Education Council (BTEC)

Central House, Upper Woburn Place, London WC1H 0HH; 0171
413 8400

BTEC offers nationally recognised qualifications through colleges, schools, universities and some in-company training centres.
There are courses available whether you are just starting your
career or are already a manager; whether you are unqualified or
seeking additional qualifications.

Qualifications offered are as follows.

BTEC First Certificate and Diploma
No formal entry requirements are needed. Both courses last one
year, the Certificate through part-time study and the Diploma
full-time.

Equivalents are GCSE grade D and below; Intermediate GNVQ;
NVQ Level 2.

BTEC suggest their First Certificate/Diploma in Business and
Finance would fit you for this type of work: building society;
clerical; insurance; office-based; receptionist; secretarial; selling;
word processing.

Core subjects studied:
  Business World – how organisations are structured; business and the community; organisations and customers.
  Administrative Systems and Procedures – storing and finding information; communications skills; word processing; health and safety; business relationships.
  Business Resources and Procedures – financial, physical and human resources; basic accounting; measuring efficiency.
  People in Business – roles, rights and responsibilities; individual career plan.

There are a number of additional options, which vary according to the centre used and your own preferences.

BTEC National Certificate and Diploma
No formal entry requirements, but you would find a BTEC First or equivalent a help. These are two-year courses, part-time or full-time, respectively.

They are equivalent to A levels, Advanced GNVQs, NVQ Level 3, or relevant work experience.

Career prospects suggested include: accounting; administration; banking; insurance; local government and Civil Service; marketing; personnel; secretarial work.

Compulsory subjects are:
  Business Structures and Goals
  Business Environment – UK business structure; role of government; banking and financial sector; international trade.
  Marketing Process – evaluating markets; market research; responding to market pressures; a marketing plan.
  Physical Resources – buildings, materials and communications systems.
  Financial Resources – preparing a budget; interpreting financial statements; a company's financial needs.
  Human Resources – personnel management; appraisals; training and discipline; planning and time management.
  Administrative Systems – roles and responsibilities; communications and administrative systems; information technology.
  Innovation and Change – factors that cause change and its impact on people.

BTEC Higher National Certificate (HNC) and Higher National Diploma (HND)

No formal entry requirements, but you must be 18 and to have obtained a BTEC National or equivalent, or had relevant work experience, would be helpful to you.

These are two-year courses, as for Nationals, and are thought of as pass-degree level (and may exempt you from first year at university). You can obtain a general Business qualification, or specialise in Finance, Marketing or Personnel.

Core modules are:

Market Relations – others in the market; factors affecting production and marketing; market information and its uses.

Operating Environment – economic, political, social factors; environmental pressures and new technology; competition and regulation.

Managing People and Activities – styles of management; factors influencing effectiveness; motivation and team building; management systems.

Managing Finance and Information – understanding and applying concepts, theories and systems; financial information management.

Organisation Structures and Processes – and how to evaluate them.

Planning and Decision-making – business planning; decision-making; contingency planning.

To these six subjects must be added ten options, either towards your speciality, or to add further skills, such as languages, law, taxation and advertising.

In addition, you will polish up 'common skills', such as: managing and developing yourself; working with and relating to others; communicating; managing tasks and solving problems; applying numeracy, technology, design and creativity.

BTEC Continuing Education

This scheme offers a short, flexible way of updating your skills and improving your knowledge of new technology or management techniques. All you need is work experience. Courses may last from a few days to several months.

BTEC GNVQs and NVQs

BTEC have developed GNVQs in Business and Information Technology and NVQs in Administration. The core syllabus is in accordance with national guidelines, see page 44. However, the options available differ widely from those offered by, say, RSA (see page 47 ff). This provides another means of broadening your personal choice of subjects.

At GNVQ Intermediate Level (GCSE grades A–C equivalent), options are:

Operating Administrative Systems – typical business organisation; office services and equipment; reception; meetings; travel and accommodation.

Financial Recording – recording and monitoring simple financial transactions; calculating wages and salaries; stock recording and control.

Information for business in Europe – currency transactions; comparison of costs; rights and responsibilities of business travellers.

Selling – investigation and analysis of retail selling methods; attracting and retaining customers; selling skills; customer care.

Other alternatives may be available at the school or college of your choice, such as: production systems; business enterprise; personal finance; retail practice.

At GNVQ Advanced Level, the options include:

Business Law

Financial Services – needs and services of different organisations; obtaining capital; competing alternative financial services.

Production – production methods; purchasing; production design; marketing; finance and personal coordination; a production plan.

Design – various techniques; customer needs analysis; preparing a design to a brief.

Business within Europe – special skills needed; economic and social trends; identifying potential; how to establish new markets.

Behaviour at Work – management influence; attitude and style.

GNVQs are meant to be broad-based and to give you the maximum opportunity to choose what attracts and suits you most.

Further Points of Interest

BTEC say that over 1,000 schools, colleges and universities offer their courses across England, Wales and Northern Ireland – so there should be one near you.

They note that only 5 per cent of BTEC National Diploma students were still looking for jobs after six months in 1994 (the latest available date), against a national average of 16.7 per cent. That is a good measure of the value of a nationally recognised qualification.

They also note that 57 per cent of National Diploma students moved on to higher education in 1993.

Ask about BTEC awards at your local college, school or sixth form, university, Careers Guidance Office or TEC.

Scottish Vocational Education Council (SCOTVEC)

Hanover House, 24 Douglas Street, Glasgow G2 7NQ; 0141 248 7900 (Publications Unit; 0141 242 2168)

SCOTVEC is the national body in Scotland responsible for developing, awarding and accrediting vocational qualifications. It works in partnership with all sectors of industry, government, schools, colleges and training organisations to provide qualifications which are relevant to employment needs.

All SCOTVEC courses are now based on a system of individual units of study, each requiring achievement of a series of skills, or 'competences'. SCOTVEC qualifications are highly flexible. They can be taken by anyone, throughout life, at school, college, or in or out of the job market. They are suitable for all levels of experience and ability, from basic to advanced professional level and include people with learning difficulties. They develop vocational skills: that is, those relevant to work.

There are three kinds of SCOTVEC unit: National Certificate Modules; Higher National Units and Workplace Assessed Units, each of which can be taken separately and listed on an individual's Record of Education and Training (RET). So your personal achievements all count, whether or not they are developed into a full qualification.

Each unit takes about 40 hours of study, which can be full- or part-time, day release, evening classes, open learning, distance learning or flexi-study. Application for entry should be made to the centre at which you wish to study.

The full set of SCOTVEC awards are:

National Certificate Modules

Forty-hour courses, run at schools, colleges and training centres (including company training centres). There are over 3,000 modules, so you can choose those subjects you require for, say, secretarial work, and those that particularly interest you in other fields. National Certificate Modules can also provide you with a basis for further study at college or university and for the advanced examinations of some professional bodies.

Modules may be taken alongside, or as an extension of, a standard, secondary-education programme at school; as part of a Technical and Vocational Education Initiative (TVEI), or as part of a Government or LEC Training scheme, or by adults seeking new skills or re-training.

Modular programmes, for both full-time and part-time students and trainees, take account of the needs of the learners and of a wide range of users, including employers in industry and commerce, institutes of advanced and higher education, professional and technician bodies, trade associations and statutory bodies.

Programmes can include any number and any combination of modules. In practice, a student's choice will be limited by various factors such as:

1. the range of modules offered by the centre where the learner is studying;
2. the vocational requirements of the learner's employment;
3. the possible need to include specific modules for statutory or registration purposes.

Skillstart

Made up of National Certificate Modules, Skillstart 1 offers slower learners a chance to gain a qualification which recognises their abilities, while Skillstart 2 is to help those without formal qualifications to improve their prospects of employment or further education.

National Certificate Clusters

These are a development of National Certificate Modules, whereby you can take three modules from a single vocational area, which can be planned to provide some of the competences required for a General SVQ. Clusters are available at three levels of difficulty.

General SVQs

Available in schools, colleges and training centres, these are especially suitable for 16–19 year-olds in school, or for adults returning to work.

They are broadly based, so providing a wide range of job skills, helpful if you are not quite sure what you want to do, or a channel through which to approach higher education.

General SVQs are available at three levels of difficulty, made up of either 12 or 18 National Certificate Modules. At Levels 2 and 3 you can get a Merit grade for excellence. Achieving an Advanced Level award is a recognised step towards study for an HNC or HND, see below.

Five 'core skills', at different levels of difficulty, are compulsory features of each General SVQ: communication; information technology; personal and interpersonal skills; numeracy; problem-solving.

Higher National Certificate (HNC) and Higher National Diploma (HND)

HNCs and HNDs can be taken at colleges, and at some universities, see page 75, on a part-time, full-time or open learning basis. Aspiring students should have completed an appropriate National Certificate, or its equivalent, although in some cases their higher secondary education awards will be sufficient. Maturity and experience may also be considered favourably by the college concerned.

These qualifications are highly regarded and recognised by many professional bodies. They are also accepted for university admission, often gaining exemption from the first and even second year of a degree programme. They are made up of from 12 to 30 Higher National Units. Each of these units is separately entered on your RET, to be added to later, or not, as circumstances dictate. So, even if you cannot complete an HNC/HND for some reason, you will be credited with whatever you *do* achieve.

Courses in the Secretarial and Office Work field include, with sample units:

HNC in Office Administration
   Communication Skills
   Interpretation of Financial Data
   The Structure of Business Organisations
   Office Administration
   Using Information Technology in Business

Producing Business Documents
Taking and Processing Shorthand (1-5)
Business Law
Public Administration

HND in Information and Office Management
Developing Personal Effectiveness
Preparing Financial Forecasts
Collection and Analysis of Numerical Data
Office Management
Business Information Management
Producing Complex Business Documents
Retail Travel Operations

HNC Business Administration
Sample modules, arranged in Competences:
  Personal Competence: Communication Skills
                            Developing Personal Effectiveness
  Administrative/Enabling: Interpretation of Financial Data
                            Working with People and Teams
  Environment: The Structure of Business Organisations
                Domestic Economic Environment
  Functional: Marketing
               Purchasing and Operations Management
  Sectoral: Office Administration

HND Business Administration
Developing Personal Effectiveness (Personal)
Interpretation of Financial Data (Administrative/Enabling)
Preparing Financial Forecasts (Administrative/Enabling)
Utilising the Computer Resource (Administrative/Enabling)
Working with People and Teams (Administrative/Enabling)
Managing Change (Administrative/Enabling)
The Structure of Business Organisations (Environment)
Domestic Economic Environment (Environment)
Business Law (Environment)

Diploma in Management Support Services
The Diploma aims to provide the skills and competence required
to manage and organise the office and associated administrative
support services available to members of an organisation, to
develop management techniques, including making full use of

information technology and to develop the ability to adapt readily to change in the workplace.
Examples of units are:
  Using Information Technology in Business
  Analysing the Organisational Environment
  Managing People
  Office Management
  Personal Effectiveness in Management
  Producing Business Documents.

Optional units include:
  Producing Complex Business Documents
  Taking and Processing Shorthand
  Business Information Management
  Marketing in Europe
  Marketing Analysis and Planning
  Second Language for Business.

Scottish Vocational Qualifications (SVQs)

Because SVQs, of which there are now over 500 to choose from, are based on standards set by industry, they are a guarantee of your ability to take on a job. So they are a very special type of qualification but at the same time open to people of all ages, at any time. 'Whatever your goals, an SVQ is your passport to success', says SCOTVEC.

Obviously, they are ideal for those in work developing their careers and can be taken through employers' own training programmes, as well as at colleges and training centres.

SVQs are available at five levels of difficulty and individual units can be built up over a period of time. The grades are:
  Level I: foundation and basic work activities
  Level II: a broad range of skills and responsibilities
  Level III: complex/skilled and/or supervisory work
  Level IV: managerial/specialist
  Level V: professional/senior managerial.

You receive a separate certificate upon completion of all the units for each level. This will help you get a job, qualify for promotion, or provide a springboard for further SVQs, HNC or HND, or even a degree.

SVQs are fully recognised in other areas of the UK, so you can transfer your studies, without interruption, if you so wish.

Professional Development Awards
Professional Development Awards are specially designed for those who have an HNC or HND, or a degree, or have gained work experience and wish either to build on their existing qualifications, or to make a career change.

Record of Education and Training (RET)
Students may take individual modules or units from the National Certificate catalogue, SVQs, or from the HNC/D frameworks. All modules and units achieved will be recorded on an RET, which will be issued to all students at their first registration with SCOTVEC. The RET is a computer-based system, constantly updated throughout the student's educational career. As well as recording individual modules and units achieved, the RET will show any of the group awards achieved. It also records workplace-assessed Units and recognition by industry and professional or other bodies of qualifications gained. It is in fact a career-long record of achievement.

Centres offering SCOTVEC Advanced Courses (HNC and HND) in Business Administration and/or Office Administration and/or Information Technology
Aberdeen College, Gallowgate, Aberdeen AB9 1DN
Angus College, Keptie Road, Arbroath DD11 3EA
Anniesland College, Hatfield Drive, Glasgow G12 0YE
Ayr College, Dam Park, Ayr KA8 0EU
Banff and Buchan College of Further Education, Henderson Road, Fraserburgh AB4 5GA
Bell College of Technology, Almada Street, Hamilton ML3 0JB
Borders College, Thorniedean House, Melrose Road, Galashiels TD1 2AF
Cambuslang College, Hamilton Road, Cambuslang, Glasgow G72 7NY
Cardonald College, 690 Mosspark Drive, Glasgow G52 3AY
Central College of Commerce, 300 Cathedral Street, Glasgow G1 2TA
Clackmannan College of Further Education, Branshill Road, Alloa, Clackmannanshire FK10 3BT
Clydebank College, Kilbowie Road, Clydebank G81 2AA
Coatbridge College, Kildonan Street, Coatbridge ML5 3LS
Cumbernauld College, Town Centre, Cumbernauld, Glasgow G67 1HU
Dumfries and Galloway College, Heathhall, Dumfries DG1 3QZ
Dundee College, Old Glamis Road, Dundee DD3 8LE
Elmwood College, Carslogie Road, Cupar KY15 4JB
Falkirk College of Technology, Grangemouth Road, Falkirk, Stirlingshire FK2 9AD

Fife College of Further & Higher Education, St Brycedale Avenue,
  Kirkcaldy, Fife KY1 1EX
Glasgow Caledonian University, Cowcaddens Road, Glasgow G4 0BA
Glenrothes College, Stenton Road, Glenrothes KY6 2RA
Inverness College, 3 Longmans Road, Inverness IV1 1SA
Jewel and Esk Valley College, Milton Road Centre, 24 Milton Road East,
  Edinburgh EH15 2PP
Kilmarnock College, Holehouse Road, Kilmarnock KA3 7AT
Langside College, 50 Prospecthill Road, Glasgow G42 9LB
Lauder College, Halbeath Road, Dunfermline KY11 5DY
Lewis Castle College, Stornoway, Isle of Lewis PA86 0XR
Moray College, Hay Street, Elgin IV30 1NQ
Motherwell College, Dalzell Drive, Motherwell ML1 2DD
Napier University, 219 Colinton Road, Edinburgh EH14 1DJ
North Glasgow College, 110 Flemington Street, Glasgow G21 4BX
Perth College, Brahan Building, Crieff Road, Perth PH1 2NX
Reid Kerr College, Renfrew Road, Paisley PA3 4DR
Sabhal Mor Ostaig, Teangue, Sleat, Isle of Skye IV44 8RQ
Shetland College of Further Education, Gressy Loan, Lerwick, Shetland
  ZE1 0BB
Stevenson College of Further Education, Bankhead Avenue, Sighthill,
  Edinburgh EH11 4DE
Stow College, 43 Shamrock Street, Glasgow G4 9LD
Telford College, Crewe Toll, Edinburgh EH4 2NZ
Thurso College, Ormlie Road, Thurso KW14 7EE
James Watt College of Further & Higher Education, Finnart Street,
  Greenock PA16 8HF
West Lothian College of Further Education, Marjoribanks Street,
  Bathgate EH48 1QJ

*A number of SCOTVEC courses are likely to be available on an evening-class
basis at most of the above centres and at many other centres not listed.
Education Authority offices should be able to provide information on the
availability of evening classes in their area. Several Education Authorities
publish a prospectus of evening-class courses.*

ILEX (Paralegal Training) Ltd (Ilex PT)
Kempston Manor, Kempston, Gedford MK42 7AB; 01234 840373

Ilex PT provides courses in law for non-lawyers, for the Certificate and Diploma of the Institute of Legal Executives. These offer
legal training to all those working, or seeking to work, in areas
where knowledge of law is required – not only in solicitors' offices.
  Ilex PT has three qualification routes: for legal secretaries;
vocational legal studies; and charity administration work. Each
route has three levels: Level II, Preparatory Business Skills, at

GCSE standard; Level III, Advanced Business Skills, GCE A level; Level IV, Management and Supervisory Skills, which is degree level. Study can be full-time, part-time, distance learning, or at a place of work, as appropriate, and is assessed by a Registered Assessment Centre (typically a college) or, for a correspondence course, by ILEX.

A feature is that assessment is entirely through the completion of a programme of assignments: six for a Core Block, from three Core Modules. There are no formal examinations.

The courses are:

Legal Secretaries Certificate, Level 2
The 'core block' modules are:
Operational skills: keyboard; audio/typewriting; word processing
Office Administration: work assignment; working with others; office machines; mail/communications; storage and retrieval; library systems
Communications skills: use of English; effective writing; telephone technique; client care; reception skills, etc.

Option modules are (one from two, if desired):
Shorthand: transcription; legal terminology; legal skills development
Information Processing: introduction to information processing; accessing data; managing databases; managing computer files and confidentiality.

Legal Secretaries Diploma and Level 3
The 'core block' modules are developments of those for Level II, while voluntary options include:
Client care; management support and Personal Assistant; advanced shorthand; advanced information processing.

Vocational Legal Studies Certificate, Level II
An open access to the study of law, where a knowledge of law and legal rights and duties is a feature of work.

The two 'core block' modules are:
The Legal Environment: nature of law; how the legal system works; how laws are made; enforcement; resolving disputes, etc
General Legal Principles: law relating to bargains in the

market-place; law relating to the workplace; land and property transactions, etc.

One module must also be selected from these three, which reflect an element of specialisation:
Retail and consumer matters; premises used for business; nature and role of criminal law.

In addition, it is recommended that students lacking experience in office work should take an Office Administration/Communications Skills double module as well. (See Legal Secretaries Certificate, above.)

Vocational Legal Studies Diploma, Level III
This course comprises a series of specialist courses, to provide a work-related specialisation, namely:

1. Welfare Benefits and Citizens' Advice, including Conveyancing
2. Company Formation
3. Debt Recovery
4. Probate
5. Insurance and Financial Services
6. Employment Matters
7. Family Issues.

Again, those lacking experience of office administration should take the Administration/Communication Skills double module as well as the specialty.

Note how these subjects are suitable both for secretarial students and for clerical workers, and open up numerous career channels.

Charity Administration, Levels II, III and Charity Law,
Level IV
As with the Vocational Studies and Legal Secretaries courses, the courses on charity administration indicate a fresh career dimension. There are thousands of registered charities and charitable trusts in the UK large enough to employ staff at different levels.
Subjects covered, in the different courses, include:
The Role of Charities in Society; Dealing with Legacies; Establishing a Charity; Charitable and non-Charitable Sta-

tus, plus the important Administration/Communications double module that is virtually indispensable to all ILEX course students, unless they are experienced.

Becoming a Legal Executive?
The ILEX PT courses are capable of providing a route into the Legal Executive stream, if you wish to attempt to qualify later. Legal Executives are qualified, experienced lawyers, with recognised status within the legal profession, and belong to the Institute of Legal Executives.

The Institute of Agricultural Secretaries and Administrators

NAC, Stoneleigh, Kenilworth, Warwickshire CV8 2LZ; 01203 696592

If you are interested in working in the countryside, a career in Rural Business Administration is an increasingly important option. It is a career with many and varied opportunities, involving such matters as keeping farm accounts accurately, supplying information on farming activities and recording livestock and crop development. Monitoring cash-flow against budget is naturally a vital part of the work, as well as payroll and contracts of employment.

There are three main types of job: Resident Farm Secretary, for one farm or estate, working closely with a farm manager; Mobile Farm Secretary, working for several farms and very much on your own; Farm Secretarial Bureaux, rather like temping in town, in that you will have a variety of jobs, as they arise.

Recognised courses:

BTEC National Diploma in Business Studies for Agricultural Secretaries (ND)
A two-year, full-time course.

SCOTVEC National Certificate for Farm Secretaries
A two-year, full-time course.

National Certificate for Farm Secretaries (NCFS)
One-year, full-time course.

Higher National Diploma in Agri-business (HND)
A two-year, full-time course.

Colleges offering these courses
Enquiries should be addressed initially to the Principal.

NCFS	Bicton College of Agriculture East Budleigh, Budleigh Salterton, Devon EX9 7BY
HND	Bishop Burton College of Agriculture Bishop Burton, Beverley, N Humberside HU17 8QG
NCFS/ND	Brooksby College Brooksby, Melton Mowbray, Leicestershire LE14 2LJ
ND and HND	Easton College Easton, Norwich, Norfolk NR9 5DX
SCOTVEC	Elmwood College Carslogie Road, Cupar, Fife KY15 4JB
NCFS	Hadlow College of Agriculture & Horticulture Hadlow, Tonbridge, Kent TN11 0AL
NCFS/ND	Kirkley Hall College Ponteland, Newcastle upon Tyne, Northumberland NE20 5AQ
ND and HND	Lincolnshire College of Agriculture & Horticulture Riseholme Hall, Riseholme, Lincoln LN2 2LG
NCFS, ND and HND	Sparsholt College Hampshire Sparsholt, Winchester, Hampshire SO21 2NF
NCFS	West Sussex College of Agriculture and Horticulture North Heath, Pulborough, West Sussex RH20 1DL

Association of Medical Secretaries, Practice Administrators and Receptionists Ltd (AMSPAR)
Tavistock House North, Tavistock Square, London WC1H 9LN;
0171 387 6005

A caring person, who enjoys working with and for others, might well consider a career as Medical Secretary, Practice Management or Receptionist. All require specialist training, especially for secretaries in hospital specialties.

AMSPAR's courses are highly flexible. Both the Secretarial and Receptionist Diplomas can be achieved by accreditation of units of competence, while the Practice Management Diploma can be done through a modular programme.

Diploma in Health Services Reception
1. A one-year, full-time course for school-leavers possessing two GCSEs, including English, wishing to work as receptionists in

any section of the Health Service. This includes general medical and dental practices, hospitals (including ward and medical record clerks), opticians and FHSA staff. Also an 18-week full-time course for mature candidates aged 19 or over.
2. A part-time course for those with relevant experience, or in post, who wish to expand their knowledge and skill to obtain the AMSPAR's Diploma in Health Services Reception.

Diploma for Medical Secretaries
1. A two-year, full-time course for those with four GCSEs, Grade A–C, one of which must be English (or at the discretion of the college).
2. A one-year, full-time course for candidates with A-level passes.

Single-Subject Examinations
Candidates for the above courses may take one or two papers at a time, on full-time, part-time or home-study basis and put them towards the Diploma.

Mature and External Candidates
Mature candidates without the prescribed entrance qualifications but with experience in the health field, or with shorthand and typewriting skills, and practising medical secretaries and receptionists unable to attend an approved course, can be accommodated, by individual assessment of their cases, into Diploma and Reception courses or a home-study course, respectively.

Diploma in Practice Management
Candidates should be employed in General Practice and hold one of the following qualifications:

1. AMSPAR Diploma in Secretarial Studies
2. Certificate in Medical Secretarial Studies
3. Certificate in Medical Reception plus one year's experience
4. Diploma in Health Services Reception
5. Certificate in Health Services Reception
   Or have a minimum of three years' experience in general practice employment
   Or have suitable managerial experience in another field

College Courses
Medical Secretarial: MS
Health Services Reception: MR
Practice Management: PM

Greater London

MS — City & East London College
Willen House, 8/26 Bath Street, London EC1V 9PL

MR — City & East London FHSA
St Leonard's Hospital, Nuttal Street, Kingsland Road,
London N1 5LZ

MS/MR — City of Westminster College
25 Paddington Green, W2 1NB

PM/MR — Ealing, Hammersmith and Hounslow FHSA
1 Armstrong Way, Southall, Middlesex UB2 4SA

MS/PM — Hammersmith & West London College
Gliddon Road, Barons Court, W14 9BL

PM — Kensington, Chelsea & Westminster FHSA
Grove House, 88-94 Westbourne Grove, London W2 5XB

MR/PM — Cherith Simmons Management
7 The Avenue, Sunbury on Thames, Middx TW16 5HU
(for Barnet FHSA; Brent & Harrow FHSA; Hillingdon
FHSA; Lambeth, Southwark, Lewisham Health Agency)

MS — South East London College
Breakspears Road, Lewisham Way, SE4 1UT

PM — Southgate College
High Street, Southgate, London N14 6BS

MS/MR — South Thames College
Tooting Broadway, London SW17 0TQ

MS/MR — Uxbridge College
Park Road, Uxbridge, Middlesex UB8 1NQ

Avon

MS/PM — City of Bath College of Further Education
Avon Street, Bath BA1 1UP

Bedfordshire

MS/MR — Barnfield College
Rotherham Avenue, Luton LU3 2AX

MS/PM — Luton College of Higher Education
Park Square, Luton LU1 3JU

Berkshire

PM — Bracknell College
Wick Hill, Sandy Lane, Bracknell RG12 2JG

Buckinghamshire
MS/MR   Aylesbury College of Further Education
                    Oxford Road, Aylesbury HP21 8PD

Cambridgeshire
MS/MR   Peterborough Technical College
                    Park Crescent, Peterborough PE1 4DZ

Channel Islands
MS   The Jersey General Hospital Teaching/Post Graduate
                    Unit
                    Gloucester Street, St Helier, Jersey

MS   Highlands College
                    PO Box 1000, St Saviour, Jersey

Cheshire
MS/MR   Macclesfield College of Further Education
                    Park Lane, Macclesfield SK11 8LF

MS/PM   Warrington Collegiate Institute
                    Winwick Road Campus, Winwick Road,
                    Warrington WA2 8QA

MS/MR/PM   West Cheshire College of Further Education
                    Eaton Road, Handbridge, Chester CH4 7ER

Cleveland
MS/MR   Cleveland Tertiary College
                    Corporation Road, Redcar TS10 1EZ

MS   Kirby College
                    Roman Road, Middlesbrough TS5 5PJ

MS/MR/PM   Stockton/Billingham Technical College
                    The Causeway, Billingham TS23 2DB

Cornwall
MS   Cornwall College
                    Pool, Redruth TR15 3RD

MS/MR   St Austell College of Further Education
                    Palace Road, St Austell PL25 4BW

Cumbria
MS/PM/MR   Furness College
                    Howard Street, Barrow-in-Furness LA14 1NB

Derbyshire
MS/MR   Chesterfield College of Technology and Arts
                    Infirmary Road, Chesterfield S41 7NG

MR   Derby Tertiary College
Greenwich Drive South, Mackworth, Derby DE3 4FW

MS/MR   South East Derbyshire College
Mundy Street, Heanor DE7 7DZ

Devon
MS/MR   East Devon College of Further Education
Bolham Road, Tiverton EX16 6SH

MS/MR   Plymouth College of Further Education
Paradise Road, Devonport, Plymouth PL1 5QG

Dorset
PM   Bournemouth and Poole College of Further Education
North Road, Parkstone, Poole BH14 0LS

MR   Weymouth College
Newstead Road, Weymouth DT4 0DX

Durham
MR   Darlington College of Technology
Cleveland Avenue, Darlington DL3 7BB

MS/MR   Derwentside College
Park Road, Consett DH8 5EE

MS/MR   New College Durham
Framwellgate Moor, Durham DH1 5ES

Essex
MS/MR/PM   Barking College of Technology
Dagenham Road, Romford RM7 0XU

MS   Basildon College of Further Education
Nethermayne, Basildon SS16 5NN

MS/MR/PM   Chelmsford College of Further Education
Upper Moulsham Street, Chelmsford CM2 0JQ

MS/MR   Colchester Institute of Higher Education
Sheepen Road, Colchester CO3 3LL

MS/MR/PM   Epping Forest College
Borders Lane, Loughton IG10 3SA

MS   Harlow College
College Square, The High, Harlow CM20 1LT

PM   South East Essex College of Arts and Technology
Carnarvon Road, Southend-on-Sea SS2 6LS

Greater Manchester

MS/MR/PM Bolton Metropolitan College
Manchester Road, Bolton BL2 1ER

MR City College Manchester
Abraham Moss Centre, Crescent Road, Crumpsall,
Manchester M8 5UF

MS/MR/PM City College Manchester
Fielden Park Centre, Barlow Moor Road,
West Didsbury, Manchester M20 8PQ

MS/MR Manchester College of Arts and Technology
City Centre Campus, Lower Hardman Street,
Manchester M3 3ER

MS Oldham College of Technology
Rochdale Road, Oldham OL9 6AA

MS/MR/PM Salford College
Walkden Road, Worsley M28 4QD

MS South Trafford College of Further Education
Manchester Road, West Timperley, Altrincham WA14
5PQ

MS Stockport College of Technology
Wellington Road South, Stockport SK1 3UQ

MS/PM Tameside College of Technology
Beaufort Road, Ashton-under-Lyne OL6 6NX

PM Tameside College of Technology
Caring and Personal Services
Stockport Road, Hyde, Greater Manchester SK14 5EZ

Hampshire

MS/MR Eastleigh College of Further Education
Chestnut Avenue, Eastleigh SO5 5HT

MS/MR/PM Farnborough Technical College
Boundary Road, Farnborough GU14 6SB

MS/MR/PM Highbury College of Technology
Cosham, Portsmouth PO6 2SA

MS/MR The Isle of Wight College
Medina Way, Newport, Isle of Wight PO30 5TA

Herefordshire

MS/MR/PM Herefordshire College of Technology
Folly Lane, Hereford HR1 1LS

Hertfordshire

MS/PM Hertford Regional College
     Broxbourne Centre, Turnford, Broxbourne EN10 6AF

MS/PM/MR North Herts College
     Cambridge Road, Hitchin SG4 0JD

MS/MR West Herts College, Cassio Campus
     Langley Road, Watford WD1 3RH

Humberside

MS/MR East Yorkshire College
     St Mary's Walk, Bridlington YO16 5JW

MR   Grimsby College of Technology & Arts
     Nun's Corner, Grimsby DN34 5BQ

MR   North Lindsey College
     Kinsway, Scunthorpe DN17 1AJ

Kent

MS/MR Bexley College
     Tower Road, Belvedere DA17 6JA

MS/MR/PM Canterbury College of Technology
     New Dover Road, Canterbury CT1 3AJ

MS/PM South Kent College
     Shorncliffe Road, Folkestone CT20 2NA

MS/MR/PM West Kent College
     Brook Street, Tonbridge TN9 2PW

Lancashire

MS/MR/PM Blackburn College
     Fielden Street, Blackburn BB2 1LH

PM   Blackpool and The Fylde College
     Ashfield Road, Bispham FY2 0HB

MR   Burnley College
     Shorey Bank, Ormerod Road, Burnley BB11 2RX

MS/MR/PM Lancaster & Morecambe College of Further Education
     Morecambe Road, Lancaster LA1 2TY

MS/MR Nelson & Colne College
     Scotland Road, Nelson BB9 7YT

MR   Preston College
     St Vincents Road, Fulwood, Preston PR2 4UR

MS/MR   Runshaw Tertiary College
Leyland, Preston PR5 2DQ

MS   Wigan College of Technology
PO Box 53, Parsons Walk, Wigan WN1 1RS

MR   Wigan and Leigh College
Marshal Street, Leigh WN7 4HX

Leicestershire
MS/MR   Wigston College of Further Education
Station Road, Wigston Magna LE8 2DW

Lincolnshire
MS/PM   North Lincolnshire College
Cathedral Street, Lincoln LN2 5NG

Merseyside
MS/PM/MR Hugh Baird College of Further Education
Balliol Road, Bootle L20 7EW

MS/MR/PM Knowsley Community College
Cherryfield Drive, Kirkby, Nr Liverpool L32 8SF

MS/MR/PM Liverpool Community College
Bankfield Centre, Bankfield Road, Liverpool L13 0BQ

MS/MR   Southport College of Art and Technology
Mornington Road, Southport PR9 0TS

Norfolk
MR   Norfolk College of Arts and Technology
Tennyson Avenue, King's Lynn, Norfolk PE30 2QW

MS/PM   Norwich City College of Further and Higher Education
School of Management and Financial Services
Ipswich Road, Norwich NR2 2LJ

Northamptonshire
MS/PM   Tresham Institute of Further and Higher Education
Tresham Campus
St Mary's Road, Kettering NN15 7BS

Northumberland
MS/MR   Northumberland College of Arts and Technology
College Road, Ashington NE63 9RG

Nottinghamshire
MS   Clarendon College of Further Education
Pelham Avenue, Nottingham NG5 1AL

Oxfordshire
MR   Oxford College of Further Education
                Oxpens Road, Oxford OX1 1SA

Shropshire
MS   North Shropshire College
                College Road, Oswestry SY11 2SA

MS/MR/PM   Shrewsbury College of Arts and Technology
                London Road, Shrewsbury SY2 6PR

MS   Telford College of Arts and Technology
                Haybridge Road, Wellington, Telford TF1 2NP

Somerset
MS/MR   Bridgwater College
                Bath Road, Bridgwater TA6 4PZ

Staffordshire
MS/PM   Cannock Chase Technical College
                Stafford Road, Cannock SW11 2AE

MS/MR/PM   Stoke-on-Trent College
                The Concourse, Stoke Road, Shelton,
                Stoke-on-Trent ST4 2DG

MS/MR   Tamworth College
                Croft Street, Upper Gungate, Tamworth B79 8AE

Suffolk
MS/MR/PM   Suffolk College of Higher and Further Education
                Rope Walk, Ipswich IP4 1LT

Surrey
MS   Brooklands Technical College
                Heath Road, Weybridge, Surrey KT13 8TT

MS/MR/PM   Carshalton College of Further Education
                Nightingale Road, Carshalton SM5 2EJ

MS/MR   North East Surrey College of Technology
                Reigate Road, Ewell KT17 3DS

Sussex
MS   Chichester College
                Department of Business and Computing,
                Westgate Fields, Chichester PO19 1SB

MS   Crawley College of Technology
                College Road, Crawley RH10 1NR

MS/MR   Eastbourne College of Arts and Technology
St Anne's Road, Eastbourne BN21 2HS

MR/PM   Hastings College of Arts & Technology
Archery Road, St Leonards-on-Sea TN38 0HX

MS/MR/PM Lewes Tertiary College
Mountfield Road, Lewes BN7 2XH

MS/MR/PM Northbrook College
Broadwater Road, Worthing BN14 8HJ

Tyne and Wear
MS/MR/PM Monkwearmouth College of Further Education
Swan Street, Sunderland SR5 1EB

MS/MR/PM Newcastle College
Rye Hill Campus, Scotswood Road, Newcastle upon Tyne
NE4 7SA

Warwickshire
MS/MR   East Warwickshire College Rugby
Lower Hillmorton Road, Rugby CV21 3OS

MS/MR/PM Mid-Warwickshire College of Further Education
Warwick New Road, Leamington Spa CV32 5JE

MS   North Warwickshire College of Technology and Art
Hinckley Road, Nuneaton CV11 6BH

West Midlands
MS/MR/PM Dudley College of Technology
The Broadway, Dudley DY1 4AS

MS   Halesowen College
Wittingham Road, Halesowen B63 3NA

MS/MR   Handsworth College
The Council House, Soho Road, Handsworth,
Birmingham B21 9DP

MS/MR/PM Sandwell College
Kendrick Street, Wednesbury WS10 9ER

MS/MR/PM Solihull College
Blossomfield Road, Solihull B91 1SB

MS/MR/PM Sutton Coldfield College of Further Education
Lichfield Road, Sutton Coldfield B74 2NW

MS/MR/PM Tile Hill College of Further Education
Tile Hill Lane, Tile Hill, Coventry CV4 9SU

MS/MR   Walsall College of Technology
St Paul's Street, Walsall WS1 1XN

Wiltshire
MS/MR   Chippenham Technical College
Cocklebury Road, Chippenham SN15 3QD

PM   Swindon College of Computing & Office Technology
Regent Circus, Swindon SN1 1PT

MS/MR   Trowbridge College
College Road, Trowbridge BA14 0ES

Worcestershire
MR/PM   Evesham College of Further Education
Cheltenham Road, Evesham WR11 6LP

MS   Kidderminster College
Hoo Road, Kidderminster DY10 1LX

MS/MR/PM North East Worcestershire College
School Drive, Stratford Road, Bromsgrove B60 1PQ

Yorkshire
MR   Barnsley College
Church Street, Barnsley S70 2AX

MS/PM   Bradford and Ilkley Community College
Great Horton Road, Bradford BD7 1AY

MS   Doncaster College
Waterdale, Doncaster DN1 3EX

MS/MR/PM Huddersfield Technical College
New North Road, Huddersfield HD1 5NN

MS/PM/MR Hull College
Queen's Gardens, Kingston-upon-Hull HU1 3DG

MR/PM   Joseph Priestley College
71 Queen Street, Morley, Leeds LS27 8DZ

MS/PM/MR Keighley College
Cavendish Street, Keighley BD21 3DF

MS/MR/PM Park Lane College of Further Education
Park Lane, Leeds LS3 1AA

MS/MR/PM Rockingham College of Further Education
West Street, Wath upon Dearne, Rotherham S63 6PX

PM   Rosedale Training Services
Clifton Hospital, York

MR	Rother Valley College of Further Education Doe Quarry Lane, Dinnington, Sheffield S31 7NH
MR	Sheffield Chamber of Commerce Eversure House, 19 Cumberland Street, Sheffield S1 4PT
MR	Sheffield College Remington Road, Sheffield S5 7PB
MS	Wakefield District College (Wakefield Centre) Margaret Street, Wakefield WF1 2DH
MR	Wakefield District College (Whitwood Centre) Four Lane Ends, Castleford WF10 5NF
MS/PM/MR	York College of Further and Higher Education Dringhouses, York YO2 1UA
MR/PM	Yorkshire Coast College of Further and Higher Education Lady Edith's Drive, Scalby Road, Scarborough YO12 5RN

Northern Ireland

MS/MR	Armagh College of Further Education Lonsdale Street, Armagh BT61 7HN
MS	Belfast Institute of Further and Higher Education College of Business Studies Brunswick Street, Belfast BT2 7GX
MS/MR/PM	Belfast Institute (Rupert Stanley) Tower Street, Belfast BT5 4FH
MS	Causeway Institute of Further & Higher Education 2 Coleraine Road, Ballymoney, Co Antrim BT53 6BP
MS	East Antrim Institute of Further and Higher Education 400 Shore Road, Newtownabbey, Co Antrim BT37 9RS
MS	Limavady College of Further Education Main Street, Limavady, Co Londonderry BT49 0EX
MS/MR/PM	North East Institute of Further Education Antrim Campus, Fountain Street, Co Antrim BT41 4AL
MS/MR	North West Institute of Further and Higher Education Strand Road, Londonderry BT48 7BY

Scotland

PM	Anniesland College Hatfield Drive, Glasgow G12 0YE

PM   Elmac Management Services
Mrs Ellen MacLeod
54 Dundonald Road, Kilmarnock, Strathclyde KA3 7AT

PM   Kilmarnock Technical College
Holehouse Road, Kilmarnock, Strathclyde KA3 7AT

MR/PM   Stevenson College of Further Education
Bankhead Avenue, Sighthill, Edinburgh EH11 4DE

Wales

MS/MR   Aberdare College
Cwmdare Road, Aberdare, Mid Glamorgan CF44 8ST

MS/MR/PM   Afan College
Margam, Port Talbot, West Glamorgan SA13 2AL

MS/MR   Barry College of Further Education
Colcot Road, Barry, South Glamorgan CF6 8YJ

MS   Deeside College
Kelserton Road, Connah's Quay, Deeside, Clwyd CH5 4B

MS   East Cardiff Tertiary College
Trowbridge Road, Cardiff CF3 8XZ

MS/MR/PM   Gwent Tertiary College, Crosskeys Campus
Risca Road, Crosskeys, Gwent NP1 7ZA

MS/MR   Gwynedd Technical College
Bangor, Gwynedd LL57 2TP

MS/MR   Llandrillo College
Llandudno Road, Rhos-on-Sea, Colwyn Bay,
Clwyd LL28 4HZ

MS/MR   Pontypridd Technical College
Ynys Terrace, Rhydyfelin, Nr Pontypridd CF37 5RN

PM   Swansea College, Office Technology Department
Tycoch Road, Tycoch, Swansea SA2 9EB

MS   Yale College
Grove Park Road, Wrexham, Clwyd LL12 7AA

The Kogan Page Careers Series

This series consists of short guides (96–128 pages) to different careers for school and college leavers, graduates and anyone wanting to start anew. Each book serves as an introduction to a particular career and to jobs available within that field, including details of training qualifications and courses. The following 'Careers in' titles are available in paperback or new editions are in preparation. Enquiries phone 0171 278 0433.

Accountancy (*5th edition*)
Architecture (*4th edition*)
Art and Design (*6th edition*)
Banking and Finance
   (*4th edition*)
Catering and Hotel Management
   (*4th edition*)
Environmental Conservation
   (*6th edition*)
Fashion (*3rd edition*)
Film and Video (*4th edition*)
Hairdressing and Beauty
   Therapy (*6th edition*)
Journalism (*6th edition*)
The Law (*7th edition*)
Marketing, Advertising and
   Public Relations (*5th edition*)
Medicine, Dentistry and Mental
   Health (*6th edition*)

Nursing and Related Professions
   (*6th edition*)
Police Force (*4th edition*)
Publishing and Bookselling (*2nd edition*)
Retailing (*5th edition*)
Secretarial and Office Work
   (*7th edition*)
Social Work (*5th edition*)
Sport (*5th edition*)
Teaching (*5th edition*)
Television and Radio (*5th edition*)
The Theatre (*5th edition*)
The Travel Industry (*5th edition*)
Using Languages (*6th edition*)
Working Outdoors (*5th edition*)
Working with Animals
   (*6th edition*)
Working with Children and
   Young People (*6th edition*)

Also Available from Kogan Page

Great Answers to Tough Interview Question: How to Get the Job You Want (3rd edition), Martin John Yate

How to Pass A Levels and GNVQs (3rd edition), Howard Barlow

How to Pass Graduate Recruitment Tests, Mike Bryon

How to Pass Selection Tests, Mike Bryon and Sanjay Modha

How to Pass Technical Selection Tests, Mike Bryon and Sanjay Modha

How to Pass the Civil Service Qualifying Tests, Mike Bryon

How You Can Get That Job!: Application Forms and Letters Made Easy, Rebecca Corfield

How to Win as a Part-Time Student, Tom Bourner and Phil Race

Job Hunting Made Easy (3rd edition), John Bramham and David Cox

Making it in Sales: A Career Guide for Women, Mary J Foster with Timothy R V Foster

Manage Your Own Career, Ben Bell

Preparing Your Own CV, Rebecca Corfield

Readymade Job Search Letters, Lynn Williams

Test Your Own Aptitude, (2nd edition), Jim Barrett and Geoff Williams

Working Abroad: The Daily Telegraph Guide to Working and Living Overseas (18th edition), Godfrey Golzen

Working for Yourself: The Daily Telegraph Guide to Self-Employment (15th edition), Godfrey Golzen

Your First Job (2nd edition), Viven Donald and Ray Grose